I'VE BEEN WONDERING

WONDERING

conversations with young theologians

I've Been Wondering

conversations with young theologians

Richard B. Steele

ATLANTA · LONDON · HYDERABAD

Paternoster Publishing
We welcome your questions and comments.

USA   PO Box 444, 285 Lynnwood Ave, Tyrone, GA, 30290
       www.authenticbooks.com
UK   9 Holdom Avenue, Bletchley, Milton Keynes, Bucks, MK1 1QR, UK
       www.authenticmedia.co.uk
India Logos Bhavan, Medchal Road, Jeedimetla Village, Secunderabad
       500 055, A.P.

I've Been Wondering
ISBN-13: 978-1-932805-68-0
ISBN-10: 1-932805-68-0

All Scripture quotations, unless otherwise indicated, are taken from the New Revised Standard Version Bible, copyright 1989, Division of Christian Education of the National Council of the Churches of Christ in the United States of America. Used by permission. All rights reserved.

Library of Congress Cataloging-in-Publication Data

Steele, Richard B., 1952-
    I've been wondering : conversations with young theologians / Richard B. Steele.
    p. cm.
    ISBN-13: 978-1-932805-68-0 (pbk.)
    1. Theology. I. Title.
    BT10.S74 2007
    230--dc22
                                        2006026807

Cover design: Paul Lewis
Editorial team: KJ Larson, Tom Richards, Megan Kassebaum

Printed in the United States of America

Dedication

I gratefully dedicate this book to those great teachers who have
most deeply shaped my work, my faith, and my life:

Richard Bernstein, Haverford College
Stanley Hauerwas, Duke Divinity School
Paul Holmer, Yale Divinity School
Robert Masson, Marquette University
James Wm. McClendon, Jr., Fuller Theological Seminary
Henri Nouwen, Yale Divinity School
Philip Rossi, SJ, Marquette University
Les Steele, Seattle Pacific University
Douglas Steere, Haverford College

Contents

Preface

This book asks how the study of Christian theology—scripture, church history, doctrine, and ethics—affects our minds and hearts. My hope is that this study deepens our faith in God, expands our intellectual horizons, and addresses our highest spiritual yearnings. But along the way it often challenges our comfortable assumptions and casts doubt on our certainties. There is both excitement and exasperation in theological inquiry. As you read this book, you will observe both. You may *experience* both, too. What you have here is a collection of email exchanges between my students and me on assorted religious and moral subjects. Some theological works tell you what the author thinks you should know. In contrast, this book contains my rough-and-ready answers to various questions that my students have actually *asked*. This isn't a theological textbook but a record of many spontaneous conversations. The student voice, which is usually muted in works of academic theology, comes through loud and clear. It may help you to understand this book if I say a bit about myself, about my school and its students, and about how a stack of random correspondence between my students and me got turned into a book.

I'm a theologian. I was raised in the church, and for as long as I can remember, I've been curious about God. I majored in philosophy in college and went straight on to seminary. I planned to do a doctorate in theology and find a teaching position. But during seminary I discovered that I had been using my religious curiosity to keep God at arm's length. I realized I had to acquire a living faith before I dared to become a teacher of theology.

My "conversion" during seminary taught me that religious curiosity isn't the same as authentic faith. But it also taught me that curiosity can be a point of entry into faith, and that if people's religious questions aren't given free expression, the result isn't authentic faith, but mindless superstition or bitter skepticism. So I encourage my students to voice their religious experiences and questions openly.

I am a professor of theology at Seattle Pacific University in Seattle, Washington. SPU is a very self-consciously *Christian* university: all of its faculty are practicing Christians. Most are Protestants or evangelicals, but there are also some Anglicans, Roman Catholics, and Eastern Orthodox. Thus, SPU is more explicitly *confessional* than most colleges and universities today, even more than those with historic ties to the church. Yet it is more intentionally *ecumenical* than many other evangelical

Christian institutions of higher learning. Our students need not be Christians, though most are.

The Free Methodist Church, the denomination that founded SPU in 1891, is one of several Wesleyan Holiness churches that sprang up in the mid-nineteenth century. Two aspects of the Holiness tradition are especially relevant to SPU—and to this book. First, it has always emphasized vital Christian experience and disciplined Christian living. Holiness folks followed John Wesley, the founder of Methodism, in teaching that to *know* God is to *feel* and *obey* God. Saving faith isn't just a matter of accepting the pardon for our sins that Christ purchased on the cross. It's also a matter of sharing in the joy of his resurrection and undergoing profound spiritual and moral transformation by the power of his indwelling Holy Spirit. Second, the early Holiness folks were social radicals. They opposed slavery, abolished pew rents (a practice that created class barriers within congregations), advocated the rights of women and ethnic minorities, and shared the gospel with those on the margins of society, such as alcoholics, prostitutes, and the unemployed. Today, only about 5% of our faculty and students are Free Methodists, but these two aspects of the Holiness ethos still mark life at SPU. The first accounts for our strict lifestyle standards, and the second for our commitment to gender and racial egalitarianism, our investment in local, national, and international missions and social service programs, and our efforts to recruit students and new faculty from underserved ethnic groups.

SPU offers a full spectrum of courses in the arts, the humanities, and the social and natural sciences. We encourage free intellectual inquiry in all disciplines. We believe that the search for truth is an act of intellectual worship, pleasing to God. Yet we also believe that God's ultimate truth, namely the truth about himself, isn't discoverable by human reason alone, but is disclosed to us in the life, death, and resurrection of Jesus Christ. And although divine self-revelation transcends human reason, it doesn't finally contradict, nor can it ever be falsified by, anything that human reason may discover about the created universe. True, the Christian gospel often challenges human illusions and pretensions. It calls us to repent of those actions and attitudes that harm ourselves, our neighbors, and our world. And it demands of us humble faith, generous love, and confident hope—virtues that are constitutive of a well-lived and fully human life, but which only divine grace can furnish. Yet the gospel does not imply that knowledge of God and knowledge of creation are mutually exclusive. Rather, it invites and empowers us to use our minds and imaginations faithfully, lovingly, and hopefully—to the glory of God and for the welfare of our neighbors.

Nevertheless, the experience of studying at a Christian liberal arts university creates fears in many students. Some are afraid that scientific inquiry and aesthetic creativity will erode their Christian faith. Others fear just the opposite, that Christian faith will stifle their love for science and art. One of my tasks is to help both groups work through these fears.

The fear that faith and knowledge are incompatible is not, however, the only spiritually troubling matter to arise for undergrads as they study theology. Indeed, it is precisely when we realize that faith authorizes the quest for knowledge, and conversely, that knowledge refines and chastens the manner in which faith is construed and practiced, that a host of other pressing questions crop up: "What does God want of my life—and what happens if God's will doesn't match my own hopes and dreams? How should I pray—and what happens if I mature spiritually to the point that I no longer feel at home in my home church? How shall I read Scripture and understand the Gospel—and what happens if my new interpretive skills and maturing religious opinions clash with what my parents believe, and with what they expected me to imbibe at a 'Christian college'? How does my faith impact my views on career, money, friendship, sex? How should I respond to the staggering evils and bewildering complexities of the world?" Students don't cordon off what they learn in theology from the rest of their lives. They seem to understand intuitively that theology is "self-involving," that it pertains to matters which concern people ultimately, and therefore concern us passionately.

Discussing such matters with my students is a way of teaching theology *theologically*. I see it as an appropriate mode of theological inquiry itself to offer vocational guidance, spiritual direction and personal counseling to my students. Mostly I do this in informal, face-to-face settings—chats in my office or the campus café. But occasionally it takes written form, when a student writes me an email *after* class about some matter that arose *in* class, which prompted further reflection or related to some burning issue in his or her life.

It wasn't my intention, when I began saving some of my email exchanges with students back in 1997, to publish them. I had a vague notion that some of what I wrote in response to student inquiries might eventually be useful in my own scholarly work. But it was my colleague and dean, Les Steele (no blood relation, by the way), who first suggested that this spontaneous, unedited correspondence would itself make an interesting book, precisely because it would give expression to the student "voice" in theological inquiry.

When I began pondering how to select and arrange the material, two things became clear to me. First, just as the original material had been written by and to my students, so the form and content of the whole collection had to be made in close consultation with my students. So I convened a cadre of theology majors to help me select what would best represent the religious and moral concerns of contemporary young adults. Second, we needed a criteria of selection: only those exchanges that illuminated the "soul" of Christian college students or that displayed particularly forceful reasoning or penetrating insight would be included. My student cadre readily accepted these criteria, but often disagreed among themselves as to how they applied to specific email exchanges. Most of the fun of the selection process, and much of the learning, came from those debates. Once the selection was made, I secured permission from the original authors to include their letters, promising to protect their privacy by changing their names and deleting or modifying any identifying marks. All the student authors whom I was able to contact readily gave their consent. There were only two or three whose addresses I could not ascertain, and whose permission I therefore couldn't secure.

Because none of this material was originally meant for publication, it preserves something of the spontaneity and unpredictability of the office tête-à-tête or the café bull session. The tone is informal and often confidential. The writing style is loose, reflecting the excitement or agitation generated by new ideas. Emotions often run high, especially when an "academic" topic clearly relates to some problem in the student's life. Leaps of logic are frequent—often because the student authors presume that their intended reader(s) will understand what has been left out. This artlessness is crucial to whatever charm the book may have, and I have therefore edited the original texts as little as possible. But some changes have been made. As noted, I have taken steps to preserve the anonymity of the student authors. I have also corrected errors of spelling and grammar and have re-phrased or paraphrased some awkward wordings. Occasionally, I have added a footnote to explain the context of a discussion or to clarify a point that the reader would not otherwise understand. And I have deleted routine pleasantries. But my student cadre insisted that such chitchat both reflects and creates the spirit of informality and conviviality between teacher and student, which makes the self-revealing communication possible. So I have blue-penciled whatever was blatantly obsequious or irrelevant to the issue at hand and have kept the rest.

It seemed advisable to begin the book with a general explanation of how I understand theology, so I have taken as an introduction a slightly modified version of a sermon I preached at the SPU chapel, which addresses that topic.

I hope you will take away from this book a deeper appreciation for the role of fearless intellectual inquiry in the life of faith. Here you will find evidence of the kinds of religious and moral questions that arise when fervent Christian faith is exposed to rigorous scientific criticism and when the barrier between purely "academic" questions and deeply "personal" matters is breached. Some religious people believe that their faith should not be subjected to scholarly analysis, either because they regard faith as a matter of the "heart" rather than the "head," or because they fear the spiritually corrosive effect of critical scrutiny. Conversely, some professors believe that scholarly objectivity obliges them to keep their own convictions and experiences, and those of their students, out of the classroom. I disagree with both groups. I believe that the Christian gospel can stand up to critical investigation, and that any attempt to protect ourselves from the discomforts of religious doubt is itself a manifestation of the unspoken fear that it can't. True piety and, therefore, serious theology are the enemies of obscurantism because they are the servants of God's truth. Critical inquiry into our faith may raise troubling questions at times. But in the long run, it is the only intellectually responsible route to spiritual maturity.

Acknowledgments

This book is very much a collaborative effort—as all teaching and learning is—and it is a pleasure to thank those who helped bring it into being.

My thanks go first to Les Steele, who originally suggested that I publish a selection of my email correspondence with students. Though we are not related by blood, as our names might suggest, I regard him as a brother.

The cadre of students from Seattle Pacific University who helped me select and arrange the material collected here included Rebecca Andrews, Emily Blake Coil, Timothy Murphy, James McMillan, Eric Rhoda, Shannon Smythe, and Lindsey Stewart Reiswig. Transcriptions of the correspondence, much of which had not been saved electronically, were made by Rebecca Andrews and Lindsey Reiswig, along with my teaching assistant, Kristi Woolum Nelson. Two of my other teaching assistants, Kristi Miller Fure and Melody Rivera Newburn, helped with other aspects of the book's production. Two SPU staff members, Kristin Stendera and Lynne Hall, helped me locate students who no longer lived on campus so that I could secure their permission to use their letters. Two of my cadre members, Emily Coil and Shannon Smythe, handled the correspondence with the contributors. To all of these dear friends I am very grateful.

Thanks also to Reed Davis, Marilyn Hair, Hope McPherson, Charles Scalise, Margaret Smith, Kristin Swanson, Linda Wagner and Rob Wall for their support, encouragement, and helpful suggestions.

A special word of appreciation goes to my editor, Kay Larson, who knows how to build up an author's ego while trimming down his prose—a priceless colleague!

Finally, I wish to express my appreciation to Seattle Pacific University, not only for being the kind of educational institution that encourages the close interaction between students and faculty that is reflected in these pages, but also for awarding me a Senior Faculty Grant during spring 2006, which enabled me to bring this project to conclusion.

Stalking the Cat:
An Introduction to
the Craft of Theology[1]

How do you become a Christian theologian? Well, for start-ers, be on your guard against theologians like me who want to talk about "theology." Why do I raise this red flag? Because the proper subject matter of theology is God—not itself. Theology is talk about God. When we talk about *talk* about God, we are not theologizing. We are engaged in something called theological method.

There's a story about the noted Christian theologian, James Gustafson, which can help us here. Gustafson taught at the University of Chicago, where the study of religion is big business, but where God himself is not always honored. One evening he went to a faculty dinner party and some of his colleagues from different fields began teasing him about his faith and his craft. "Hey, Jim," said one of them, mockingly, "say something theological." Gustafson looked at him evenly and replied, "God."[2] One word . . . one *name*: that was all he needed. And he was right: to speak theologically is to speak about *God*, not so speak about *speech* pertaining to God.

Yet even though theological method is not theology as such, to do theology well we must know something about theological method. For not all talk about God is appropriate. Far from it! So much of our preaching, our witnessing, and even our learned theologizing, is little short of blasphemy! How often do we hear sermons that treat God with such cozy familiarity, that God's "almightiness" and "holiness" and "otherness" are utterly forgotten! How often do we hear God's name invoked in what is really nothing more than a sales pitch for "our ministry" or "our church building program" or "our evangelical university" or "our side" of this or that doctrinal dispute! When we Christians thus dishonor God by trying to make God serve our purposes, is it any wonder that an unbelieving world despises the gospel? Paul Tillich, another twentieth century theologian, once wrote: "The first step to atheism is a theology which drags God down to the level of doubtful things. The game of the atheist is then very easy. For he is perfectly justified in destroying such a phantom and all its ghostly qualities."[3] Tillich makes an important point. The best way for Christians to promote atheism is to talk foolishly, cheaply, tritely, or selfishly about God. So learning to talk properly about God, and learning how not to talk improperly about God, are absolutely necessary. In other words, like it or not, we must talk about theology.

One definition of theology that I particularly like goes like this: "Theology is a blind man . . . in a dark room . . . searching for a black cat that isn't there—and finding it." Let's unpack this analogy, highlighting four characteristics of proper speech about God.

1. Humility. The first thing a theologian needs is humility. He has to realize that, with respect to God, he is quite blind. And the wiser the theologian, the more clearly he sees how blind he is. Think of that wonderful story from Mark 8 about the blind man who is healed by Jesus—yet not healed all at once, but in two distinct stages. At first he can see nothing at all. Then Jesus comes along, spits on his hand, smears the saliva on the man's eyes, and then asks him, "Do you see anything?" The man replies, "I see people; but they look like trees, walking." Jesus then lays his hands upon him a second time, and he is able to see everything clearly. The situation of the theologian is like that of the blind man during that strange moment between the first touch of Jesus and the second: more able to see than before, but only well enough to know that his sight is still blurry and out of focus. And like it or not, the theologian soon learns that he is *permanently* in that condition, at least on this side of heaven. The one thing he learns to see with absolute clarity is how badly he and everyone else needs the divine ophthalmology.

The wise theologian bears this knowledge in mind whenever she tries to describe the fruits of her research and meditation to her colleagues and students. Hence, there must always be a note of humility, caution, provisionality, and tentativeness to theological speech. Nothing is more absurd than a theologian who pretends to be an "expert" or "authority" on God—as if God weren't high and lifted up above all human knowing, as if God weren't elusive, mysterious, transcendent, and incomprehensible. God's judgment upon those theologians whose speech lacks proper humility has been brilliantly expressed by Karl Barth, yet another great theologian of our era, in the following humorous paraphrase of one of Amos's prophecies:

> I hate, I despise your lectures and seminars, your sermons, addresses and Bible studies, and I take no delight in your discussions, meetings, and conventions. For when you display your hermeneutic, dogmatic, ethical and pastoral bits of wisdom before one another and before me, I have no pleasure in them. . . . Take away from me the hue and cry that you old men raise with your thick books and you young men with your dissertations! I will not listen to the melody of your reviews that you compose in your theological magazines, monthlies, and quarterlies.[4]

2. Wariness. If the first quality of proper theological speech is humility, the second is what I shall call wariness. The theologian realizes not only that he is blind, but also that he is standing in a darkened room, full of dangerous obstacles. Scripture insists that our whole world is plunged into darkness. According to St. John, "The light shines in the darkness, and the darkness did not overcome it" (John 1:5). And St. Paul adds, "For once you were darkness, but now in the Lord you are light" (Ephesians 5:8). Of course, the accent on these verses falls on the dazzling light, which Christ himself is, and which he shines into our hearts and our world. That is the theologian's chief hope and joy, and I shall say something more about it in what follows. But first we must take seriously the sober warning of these verses, that we dwell in a sin-darkened world, where all kinds of snags, booby-traps, pitfalls and dangers lurk in our path.

My father once had an experience that illustrates the theologian's situation. He got up in the middle of the night to go to the toilet. He didn't want to disturb my mother's sleep by switching on the light, so he tried to feel his way to the bathroom. He circled the bed with no problem, located the dresser to his left, and then headed confidently toward the john with his arms extended ahead of him to find the door. He assumed the door was closed. But it wasn't. It was ajar, and passed untouched between his outstretched arms until it smashed him squarely on the nose.

Of course, just as all of us are spiritually blind, so all of us live in a sin-darkened world, full of invisible but ever-present hazards. But the point I especially want to stress is that there are special perils in the road of those who presume to take the Word of God upon their lips—perils for themselves, and perils set by them for those to whom they speak. For as Scripture tells us, the powers of darkness are nowhere more dangerous than when they masquerade as angels of light (2 Corinthians 11:14), as when, for instance, self-appointed "true believers" persecute heretics and unbelievers . . . or when predatory clergy sexually assault young parishioners or line their pockets with the offerings of the faithful . . . or when the wealthy and powerful assure themselves that their privileged status in the world is God's will . . . or when self-important professors of theology pontificate to their colleagues or bully their students. In short, whenever religious speech is made to serve human passions and interests, the Golden Calf has reappeared in the assembly of the Lord. It is the task of the theologian to keep vigil for such snares—and not least for those that he himself is tempted to set for others.

3. Attention. How can the theologian protect herself and her hearers from such perils? To answer that question, we must turn to a third feature of proper theological speech: silence. Now, I hope you have caught the paradox here. It is quite intentional. A true theologian is one who listens before she talks, who listens first and foremost to the Word of God, and who listens also to the questions and cries of pain which spring from her own heart and from the hearts of those around her. The theologian is one who shuts up and pays attention before she presumes to speak.

We've said that the theologian is a blind man in the process of being healed. We've said that the theologian is standing in a dark room, wary of booby-traps. Now we observe that the theologian is looking for a cat that isn't there. We must be careful here. We don't mean that the object of the theologian's quest—God himself—doesn't exist. If that were so, the theologian would be "of all people most to be pitied" (1 Corinthians 15:19). No, what we mean is that God, though everywhere present in the world, is usually hidden from all but those who look and listen with great attention. True, God sometimes reveals himself to even the blindest, unwariest, and most inattentive souls with blazing intensity. Think of the Hebrew patriarch, Jacob, who once dreamed about a ladder reaching from earth to heaven, on which the angels of the Lord were ascending and descending. Upon awakening, he exclaimed, "Surely the LORD is in this place—and I did not know it" (Genesis 28:16). So God sometimes appears to those who aren't on the lookout for him. But usually God discloses himself only to those who search for him—longingly, diligently, and persistently. That's what theology is: stalking this elusive "black cat" through the brambles and thickets of life.

Does the image of God as a black cat startle you? Well, do you recall the place in the Book of Revelation where Christ is called "the Lion of Judah" (Revelation 5:5)? Or have you read the great sermon by Jonathan Edwards called "The Excellency of Jesus Christ," in which this image of the Lion of Judah is played off against that of the Lamb of God, in order to depict the divine and human natures of the Lord? And surely you're familiar with *The Chronicles of Narnia* by C. S. Lewis, in which Aslan, the great lion, is the Christ-figure. (And by the way, in one of those novels, *The Horse and His Boy*, Aslan appears for a short time as a stray house cat.) Why the feline imagery? Maybe it's because cats have a regal bearing, and yet are very affectionate and approachable—when *they* want to be. Maybe it's because they have tremendous energy—and yet often hold it in reserve, under the outward guise of elegant repose or graceful motion. Or maybe it's because they come and go as they please—not when they are summoned.

Elizabeth Marshall Thomas, an anthropologist who studied the Bushmen of the Kalahari Desert, tells the following story: One morning, from her tent, she heard several jackals calling to one another across the veldt. "Tsa, tsa," went their sad, loud cry, which in the language of the Bushmen means, "Water, water." And then she was astounded to hear one of the Bushmen stand up and answer the jackal, imitating its voice exactly: "Tsa, tsa." It turned out that this is a kind of game or hobby for the desert folk—answering every animal and every bird with its own sound, keeping up these "conversations" for hours. Every animal, that is, except the lion. When the roar of the lion is heard, the Bushmen keep silent. "In the Kalahari," writes Dr. Thomas, "it is considered safer to let the lion have the last word."[5]

4. Praise. We have said that theology is like a blind man standing in a dark room looking for a black cat that isn't there. But now we come to the final point. Despite all these disadvantages, the blind man actually finds the cat! Or rather, the cat finds the blind man. For that's the amazing thing about God. God wants us to seek him, and God wants us to find him, but God also wants us to realize that the success of our search is finally due, not to our diligence or ingenuity in searching, but to his desire to be found. God wants us to know that we are blind—so that *he* can open our eyes. God wants us to know that we are standing in a dark room—so that *he* can be our light. God wants us to know that he is the great Lion, who always has the first and last word, but who nevertheless speaks to us and listens to us.

Thus, theological speech ends in a kind of stammering, ecstatic praise. It's the vocabulary of miracle and the grammar of mystery. It's an attempt, as someone has put it, to "eff the ineffable." It is words about the Word who spoke himself into flesh. It is language that speaks only long enough to remind us to fall silent in wonder. In the end, theology is finally doxology.[6]

So here is the sum of the matter: Proper theological speech is marked by humility, because God remains unfathomable and incomprehensible. It is marked by wariness and constant self-criticism, because it recognizes the way in which all people, and especially theologians, are tempted to exploit the truth of the gospel for selfish ends. It is marked by a certain reverent attentiveness and responsiveness to the Word of God and the cries of humanity. It always proceeds from silence and leads back into silence. Finally, it is marked by praise and thanksgiving, festivity and joy.

Let me close with a story about one of the greatest of all Christian theologians, St. Thomas Aquinas. As death was drawing near, Thomas heard the voice of the Lord: "You have spoken well of me, Thomas. What reward would you like?" "Nothing but yourself, Lord." He answered. He was able, at that moment, to make such a reply since he had previously, in his mortal life when speaking and writing of God, desired nothing but God alone. It is for that very reason that he had always spoken of him well.[7] So it was for St. Thomas. So may it be for all of us who practice the sacred science.

NOTES

1 The introductory essay is a slightly modified version of a sermon that I preached at an SPU chapel service on October 15, 1998. It was the third in a three-part series presented by the School of Theology to introduce the religion component of the new general education program that was at that time being introduced. Dr. Kerry Dearborn opened the series by explaining the freshman "Christian Formation" course. Dr. Frank Spina followed with an account of the sophomore "Christian Scriptures" course. I completed the cycle by discussing the course for upperclassmen, "Christian Theology."

2 James Gustafson, "Say Something Theological," *1981 Nora and Edward Ryerson Lecture* (Chicago: University of Chicago, 1981), 3, quoted in Stanley Hauerwas, "On Keeping Theological Ethics Theological," in *Against the Nations: War and Survival in a Liberal Society,* (Minneapolis: Winston Press, 1985), 23 and 45n.

3 Paul Tillich, "The Escape from God," in *The Shaking of the Foundations* (New York: Charles Scribner's Sons, 1948), 45.

4 Karl Barth, *Evangelical Theology: An Introduction*. Trans. Grover Foley. (New York, Chicago, San Francisco: Holt, Rinehart and Winston, 1963), 135f.

5 Elizabeth Marshall Thomas, *The Harmless People* (New York: Vintage Books, 1989), 81.

6 Cf. Geoffrey Wainwright, *Doxology: The Praise of God in Worship, Doctrine, and Life: A Systematic Theology* (New York: Oxford University Press, 1980).

7 Adapted from Jean Leclerq, *The Love of Learning and the Desire for God: A Study of Monastic Culture*, trans. Catherine Misrahi (New York: New American Library, 1962), 262f.

CHAPTER 1

"NOW THAT I AM AN ADULT . . ."

The letters in this chapter show how students readily see connections between what they learn in class and their own convictions, prejudices, ambitions, commitments, and relationships. Often, they see these connections for themselves and talk about them among themselves. But I think it is part of the teacher's job to encourage students to *look* for such connections, to share them privately with the teacher or publicly during class sessions or on a course website, and to analyze their observations rigorously as a regular course-related learning activity. "Personalizing" course material in this way not only helps students to reap greater benefit from their studies, but also to master basic information and key concepts more thoroughly and accurately.

We must be cautious, however. We are all prone to read our own experiences and viewpoints back into the texts we read, or to use the mores and conventions of our own society to evaluate the ideas and customs of other periods and cultures. We must be alert to the ways in which our own interests and presuppositions skew our understanding of texts. On the other hand, we can never achieve pure "objectivity" or "value-neutrality" when studying people different from ourselves. The right way is midway between these two extremes. Harry Stack Sullivan once observed, "We are all more truly human than otherwise." This suggests that we can and should enter imaginatively and sympathetically into the experiences of people of other times and places, searching for that common core of "humanity," which binds us all together, but seeking also for vantage points outside ourselves from which to critique our own prejudices and parochialisms.

These letters show that some students are glad to be allowed to personalize their study of theology in this way. But others find it intimidating to do so, preferring to keep themselves at a safe distance from the material—only to discover that this self-defensive strategy keeps them from facing their doubts, fears, and regrets.

One caveat here: When we are young, we sometimes indulge in melodramatic displays of religious emotion and make zealous, if not always profound or enduring, ideological commitments. Or at least I did when I was young. Usually, this passion is tempered with time. We learn that the intensity of our religious emotions is not always a good indication of the sincerity of our faith or the depth of our virtue. We learn to test our experience against the norms of Scripture and the long wisdom of the Christian tradition. We learn for ourselves what St. Paul meant when he wrote, "When I was a child, I spoke like a child, I thought like a child, I reasoned like a child; when I became an adult, I put an end to childish ways" (1 Corinthians 13:11). Thus, our theological studies become the vehicle for our spiritual transformation.

SUBJECT: HURT AND FRUSTRATION WITH
THE CHURCH

Dr. Steele:

I just wanted to thank you for making time for me to share my random thoughts and emotions with you after class. I cannot help but be a little embarrassed for crying in class, when I cannot explain why. But I do know that for the last month and a half, God has been deepening in my heart and mind, to a place I did not know existed. I have been extremely reflective on my life journey, and the 18 credits of Christian Education classes I am taking have definitely played a huge role. I received a card after class from a seminar I helped plan in the spring last year. It was focused on transitional times and each person wrote themselves a note remembering the ways God has been faithful through those times. The quote on the front of the card says, "I cannot, I must not, and I will not forget how the Lord has changed my life." And when I opened the card, I had written myself a list of the ways God has profoundly changed my life and been faithful.

My tears in class stem from a deep passion that has grown over the years, but life has tried to put out lately. The paradoxes of life can pull us in so many directions, but my desire is to go in His direction. And whatever form that takes, I will endeavor to be more the person God created me to be. My tears also stem from hurt and frustration with the church, Christians, and the world. I believe that God is allowing me to see beyond my idealistic views and see the reality of what he did and how we, as Christians, have simplified it, me included. That hurts my heart.

If I have said anything, may it simply be that I see more of who Christ calls me to be in you and the places we are going in class. I don't have answers or conclusions yet, but I have come to a place in my walk where I am now willing to bear the cross so I may know more of Christ. I am learning how to be real . . . so much that it hurts.

Thank you,

Tammy

Dear Tammy,

First, let me say that it is not at all uncommon for highly sensitive and deeply principled people like yourself to be touched at a very deep level by new insights and experiences but to be unable for a while to articulate exactly why such insights and experiences move them to tears. It is as if we have taken in more Truth than we can put into words, and our initial response is to be emotionally overwhelmed. (This, I think, is exactly what happened to the first generation of Jesus' disciples: the total impact of his teaching, his exemplary life, his sacrificial death, and his triumphant resurrection were simply more than they had words and concepts to express, and it took them a while to process the meaning and significance of all that.) As time passes, and we think and speak and pray about our experiences, things gradually come into clearer focus. This is, in one respect, a very good thing: we call it "theologizing." But it can also present a very deep temptation: to move further and further away from the primal experience into the rarefied atmosphere of conceptualization. I, for one, am pledged to stay as close to that primal experience as possible, even though, as a "professional theologian" (whatever *that* could be!) I am also called to think and speak and pray about it. At any rate, my guess is that you got in touch with some things in your own spiritual life that were more than you could express just then. Give it time: intellectual clarity does come with steady reflection on authentic spiritual experience. (And please accept my apology for asking you to speak in class before you were quite ready.)

Second, I think I understand what you mean by "hurt and frustration with the church, Christians, and the world." Obviously I don't know specifically what kinds of hurts and frustrations you have undergone, but I have undergone a fair number of these myself, and have certainly experienced feelings of sorrow and outrage at seeing the stupidity, pettiness, and selfishness of people one expects so much of. To this I would say two things: (1) That such hurts and frustrations are signs of disappointed love, and that it is far better to hold fast to that love, even though it means having to endure the pains of inevitable disappointments, than to stop loving in order to insulate oneself against disappointment. You can avoid the pains of love by becoming indifferent or cynical. But in my view the cost—a life of loveless bitterness or emotional superficiality—is simply too high. (2) In my most honest moments, I see that it is often *myself* that I expect most of, and that it is *my own* stupidity, pettiness, and selfishness that is the most galling to me. Thus my "sorrow and outrage" at others is at least partly an external projection of my interior guilt and shame. I would not presume to suggest that the same is true for you. Only God and you yourself can possibly know that. I would only say, as one for whom it *is* true, that it helps me to be more patient with others when I recognize how much of my impatience with them is really displaced impatience with myself.

Finally, let me say how much it means to me to know that you "see more of who Christ calls [you] to be in . . . the places we are going in class." That is surely what a theology class is for. Or at least that is the aim of my own approach to theology. I look forward to getting to whatever those "places" may be, and if you ever want to chat about where they are and what the journey of getting there is like, it would certainly be my honor and pleasure. Say the word, and we'll set a time to get together.

In Christian service,

RBS

SUBJECT: IS LIFE REALLY A "TEST"?

Hi Dr. Steele,

It is barely five minutes after class, and I needed to get some things off my chest. Two days ago I saw a friend I haven't seen in a couple weeks, and she told me her dad, whom I knew had cancer, was off a liver transplant list because the cancer had spread to such an extent that it was terminal, and the doctors had given him one to two years to live. This conversation took place in the cafeteria, and I was having a good day when she told me this. I was in shock to say the least, and I told her honestly that I didn't know how to respond to that. I have never lost anyone in my family or any of my loved ones, but I know one day I will. That's how life is. It showed me that I need to start looking at my own life more carefully and thank God everyday for all that he has given me.

Today's discussion almost saddened me when I started picturing life as a test to be endured before we are rewarded with heaven. Why as Christians do we have to see it this way? I have always been positive about life, when I get down it is usually over a bad grade, a girl problem or some other trivial matter which really doesn't matter if your journey with God is on schedule. I just think that my friend's example and the class discussion has made me realize that not every problem I face is the end of the world, but I shouldn't tackle every hurdle I face with that same attitude. I have many dreams in life that God helps give me. I know one day I will meet the woman of my dreams, my best friend, and the future mother of my children all rolled into one almost divine being (in my eyes at least). I know I should recover from every broken heart I experience along the way with the hope that God has a plan for me, too. I know I should fight obstacles along the path of my career both professional and personal, and that one day, my faith and hard work will be rewarded.

Sometimes, though, I sit and reflect on the last months of my life and wonder why God has made things so hard for me. Granted it is all relative, and that life seems too much for me to handle in my own eyes but not to someone else looking at how much I do have as opposed to how much I don't. But the issue is that they are my problems, and that's why they are important to me. I know I have to endure to see the rewards of my effort at the end, but sometimes I have to wonder why God has made it so hard for each and every one of us.

Regards,

Chad[1]

Dear Chad,

Thanks for writing such a powerful and eloquent message. Let me address several things you have said here:

First, I do not think there really is any "right" way to respond to news given us by friends about tragedies which they or their loved ones have endured—except perhaps to extend heartfelt sympathy to them, to promise them your prayers, and perhaps to weep quietly with them if that is appropriate to your true feelings. (It is never wise to fake the level of one's emotional reaction to another person's problems.) There are no "magic words" by which to make them "feel better," and the recitation of pious formulas usually rings strangely hollow, because it often appears to be little more than a way of making *you* feel better in the presence of someone who is suffering.

Second, there are, I suppose, different ways of understanding the idea that "life is a test to be endured before we are rewarded with heaven." One could say that in a spirit of sullen resignation, meaning by it that one just has to endure the sorrows and sufferings of today and hope for heavenly compensation later. That is not, however, what I believe or what I meant to say. I do not think of heaven as an eternal reward for heroically enduring temporal unhappiness. Rather, what I meant is that all of creation and all of history are finally in God's gracious hands, and that because we have encountered the Risen Christ we have been given an anticipatory glimpse of the glorious divine consummation of the whole cosmic and human story—a peek at the last page, as it were. This can give us confidence and courage in the here and now, not because it mitigates our present sufferings or promises deferred compensation for them, but because it sets all that happens to us in the here and now in the context of God's grand and ultimate design.

Third, the Christian tradition has been pretty consistent in *denying* that "God made [life] so hard for each and every one of us." One of the key points of the Garden of Eden story is precisely that God originally intended, and still intends, good for all of us. It is *we* who have made it hard for ourselves and each other by our disobedience. Of course, there is no direct, one-to-one correspondence between each individual's sins and his or her own sufferings. (That is closer to the Hindu concept of "karma.") On the contrary, your sins bring suffering not only to you, but also to me, just as mine do to you. Similarly, your virtues and good deeds not only bring joy to you, but also tangible and intangible benefits to me, just as, again, mine do to you. We are all in this together, for both good and ill, and rather than ascribing the difficulties of life to the deficiencies of God's administration of the universe, the Christian tradition has tended to interpret the human condition as tragically fallen through human sin, but in the process of being redeemed by divine grace. And the ethical task of the human life consists in conforming one's life to the grace that has been exemplified in the person and work of Jesus Christ and shed abroad in our hearts by the Holy Spirit.

Best regards,

RBS

SUBJECT: DO WE "PROGRESS" TOWARD GOD?

Good Day, Dr. Steele,

Starting from your lecture on the history of doctrine a couple days ago, I began to think deeply about the idea of "progress," which we discussed briefly after class that day on the way to your office. I have worked a lot out since then, and would like to share it with you sometime, and I would greatly appreciate it if you could try and help me understand or explain an obstacle I seem to have run into concerning this.

I can see how getting rid of the whole notion of progress would be very beneficial to modern thinking, and would help combat a lot of subtle problems that we have come to surround ourselves with (i.e. connections to envy, comparison, coveting, gluttony, etc.) but the only part that I am having trouble with is when I think of our "progress" to God or getting closer to God. That seems to tear down my whole argument against the notion of progress. Could you please help with trying to figure this out? Maybe either over email or by arranging a time to meet and discuss this?

Charles

Dear Charles,

First, you may want to look at Christopher Lasch's book, *The True and Only Heaven: Progress and Its Critics* (New York: W. W. Norton, 1991). It's the fullest treatment of the "myth" of progress (using "myth" here, not in the sense of "falsehood," but in the sense of "governing idea" or "unquestioned presupposition," which shapes the thinking of a large number of people).

Second, I think we might make a distinction between "progress" as a cultural myth and what I shall here call "spiritual growth" as an autobiographical fact. The former refers to the conviction that, over the past three centuries, Western society has grown demonstrably more scientifically and technologically sophisticated, culturally diverse, and economically prosperous. Obviously not everybody has shared equally, or even equitably, in the luxuries and emoluments, and there is even some evidence that the poorest layers of society are poorer and more numerous than a century ago. The "two-thirds" world, in particular, has been ravaged by the predatory lust of the West. Thus, the right-wing slogan, "a rising tide lifts all boats," is baloney. Still, there is truth in the belief that "progress" in science, industry, and technology is incremental, and perhaps even exponential. The more we have, the more we have the wherewithal to make more of whatever we want, and the more we have the incentive to think up new things for people to want.

But spiritual growth is not that way at all. Although it is true that growth in knowledge *can* go hand in hand with growth in wisdom and devotion (and if it weren't true, places like SPU would be colossal frauds!), it is also possible for people who have little academic experience to grow in grace, and for people who have a great deal of academic experience (including theological training!) to stagnate spiritually. In short, spiritual growth is not simply a matter of mastering certain bodies of information. And it is certainly not a matter of acquiring more and more shiny toys and glitzy stuff. It is a matter of deeply accepting reality and learning to discern God's work in the world and in one's own life.

Assuming this distinction is tenable, one could argue in favor of the idea of spiritual growth without having to endorse the myth of limitless technological progress and economic expansion. Does this help?

RBS

SUBJECT: LEAVING MY HOME CHURCH

Dr. Steele:

For about a year now I have been struggling with some
issues that involve my church. I was raised in a small rural
Methodist church where everyone knew anything and
everything about everyone else. It definitely portrayed
the "family church" feel that we talked about in class.
When I was in high school I went through confirmation
classes and became a member of our Methodist church.
I felt a very close bond to that church because that is
where I learned my first words about God. However, now
that I have adventured out into the bigger world I see
many doors that God has opened up for me. I now attend
a Pentecostal church where the worship and the overall
atmosphere in the church are more expressive (where
the so-called lifting of the hands is taking place). Many
people in my Methodist church consider this to be nothing
more than an attention-getting practice. My family and
I have disputes about this and my "abandonment" of
the Methodist church. I was intrigued today about what
Alison said in class about confirmation. When I decided to
go through confirmation I really wasn't sure what exactly
it entailed, and now I almost feel as if I am breaking the
vows and ties that I had to my church. But, the part that I
am struggling with is that this year I have created a clean
heart and a new passion for God, but yet I am slipping
away from my membership in my home church, but also
finding a sense of community in another. When asked
what denomination I am, I still answer Methodist, but I do

say that I attend a Pentecostal church. To me it really does not matter what denomination I am. The most important thing to me is my personal relationship with God. I am just wondering if you have any insights on how all this fits together. I am curious as to how you, being a Methodist yourself, feel about confirmation to the church and the so-called abandonment of it.

God bless,

Suzy

Dear Suzy:

Let me say two things: First, I would note the fact that Pentecostalism has deep roots in the Wesleyan-Holiness tradition, and although you may be in the process of "abandoning" the Methodist church (to use your parents' term), that need not mean that you have rejected all the values and beliefs which you imbibed from your earlier affiliation there. Of course, there are wide differences among Methodist churches—and among Pentecostal churches— and between "typical" Methodist and "typical" Pentecostal churches, so I would not want to push this point too far. And even though you may have found things in Pentecostalism that you have come to cherish deeply, and did not find in your rural Methodist congregation, there may be some merit in sharing with your folks how much of your former religious identity you have retained. That way they may see that your decision is not a rejection of your religious upbringing (and therefore an implicit judgment upon them or upon the church they love), but an attempt on your part to find something that Methodism itself taught you to desire, but for some reason could not supply.

Second, I would encourage you to think very hard about your statement: "The most important thing to me is my personal relationship with God." There is something right about this—and something very "Methodist" about it, I might add! Authentic Christian faith is, as Wesley insisted, a deeply personal thing. Yet as Wesley also insisted, "There is no Christianity but *social* Christianity." That is, Christian faith is "personal," but not individualistic. And a church that tempts its members to equate the sincerity of their faith with the emotional intensity of the religious experiences they enjoy during worship is on thin ice. I am obviously in no position to evaluate whether the Pentecostal church that you are now attending is guilty of that aberration. (And many are not guilty of it, I'm pleased to say!) But I would urge you to ask whether, in the name of finding a deeper life of faith, you are really looking for a religious "high." That might be problematic—not only on Methodist grounds, but on authentically Pentecostal grounds as well.

RBS

SUBJECT: NO LONGER CONTENT WITH SUNDAY
SCHOOL ANSWERS

Dr. Steele,

This email may seem a bit random and preemptive, since I'll be taking your UFDN 1000 Christian Formation class in the fall and haven't actually had the pleasure of meeting you in person yet. I am very good friends with quite a few students in the class, however, and have heard nothing but the most respectful and honoring things said about you—including from a few cynics in the class, who I know would not say such things lightly.

So let me explain a little bit why I'm writing you in the first place. I'm not at all what you might call a "sheltered Christian"—but I certainly have grown up in the church. My father was a pastor for the Evangelical Covenant denomination, and now works at their headquarters, overseeing new church plants. I went to Awana[2] and Sunday school and youth group and was a counselor for Vacation Bible School all the way through. I certainly was always a critical thinker about faith, and had hardly any Christian friends—and so was continually having my faith called into question. But, by and large, I felt like I held on to it pretty solidly. In 2003-04, I went to a one-year Bible college in South America, and spent the summer after working for an inner-city Christian organization in Indianapolis. I'm going to be a Student Ministry Coordinator next year.[3]

It all sounds like a very typical life journey for an SPU student, but it's really anything but. Having grown up with Buddhists and Jews and Atheists of all persuasions, I've always held to a bit more of a liberal theology than what I was raised with—which is to say, one that's a little more inclusive. Lately, though, perhaps in reaction to the overwhelming evangelical conservative Christian community at SPU, I've started backing up more and more until my theology has become quite unorthodox indeed. In fact, these are the questions—which are really basic questions to the Christian faith—that I've really started to chew on:

1. What is salvation? What are we being saved from, and for what purpose?

2. Is there a heaven or hell? Is there a reason to believe in God apart from wanting eternal paradise (or conversely, to avoid eternal damnation?) How much of our belief about heaven and hell is biblical?

3. Biblically speaking, what can we actually expect from God? Is it wrong to pray for good weather or an open parking space? Is it wrong to be upset with God when real tragedy strikes? Or, if he doesn't promise wealth, health, safety, or happiness—why believe in God?

4. What is the difference between a "blessing" and "salvation" (specifically in light of the beatitudes)?

5. Is our conception of having a "personal relationship with Jesus Christ" actually biblical? Is that actually required for salvation—whatever salvation is?

6. What is Jesus talking about when he refers to the Kingdom of God/Heaven?

7. Which does God honor more—someone who earnestly struggles and seeks and wants to have faith, but ultimately rejects it? Or someone who blindly accepts a "faith," and never questions?

I know the Sunday school answers. I know what evangelical Christianity in the United States generally says about it. But living in Ecuador, I know that, say, liberation theology answers these questions quite differently, and that Christians in the east or west, or Christians during different historical periods have answered these questions very differently. So I'm not content to say, "Well, this is what James Dobson says about this, and that's good enough for me."

Plus I'm going to be an SMC next year, and I feel like leading Bible studies in which I admit that I'm not sure if there's heaven or hell isn't really going to do anything but confuse the girls on my floor. With all these questions in mind, I've started going back through all of the gospels, and just writing down what Jesus says. I'm only at the very beginning of that process, though.

So the reason why I'm writing you is that I was wondering if you could give me just your honest, two-sentence answer to any one of those questions—just something to give me some food for thought as I work back through the gospels. I know I just bombarded you with a whole bunch of different issues—and I'm not looking for a dissertation on any one of them (after all, this is your summer, too!).

But if you could just give me a thought or two, I'd really appreciate this.

Take care,

Marissa

Dear Marissa:

You have asked all the "big" questions—and yes, each deserves a dissertation-length answer. But I shall take you at your word, and give you brief replies which, I hope, will at least be thought-provoking.

1. *What is salvation? What are we being saved from, and for what purpose?* Someone once asked G. K. Chesterton what was wrong with the world? He replied, "I am." Similarly, the cartoon character Pogo once remarked (misquoting, but significantly improving on, Commodore Perry): "We have met the enemy and he is us." Salvation happens whenever a person takes responsibility for her own brokenness (which includes the tendency to "break" others), and then decides, with God's mercy and through God's power, to seek healing for herself and to become a healer for others.

2. *Is there a heaven or hell, etc.?* I think of hell as the "place" (or "state") where you get everything you always wanted . . . only to discover that what you wanted is not nearly good enough to satisfy you for as long as you're going to possess it. Conversely, heaven is where you learn to desire the one thing that is truly worth having and where the satisfaction of that desire at each moment brings about an ever more

intense desire for it. I hardly need to tell you what the object of that salvific and unquenchable desire might be.

3. *What can we actually expect from God, etc.?* One must make a distinction here: God is absolutely faithful, but at the same time utterly unpredictable. God's faithfulness keeps us from despair; God's unpredictability keeps us from presumption. Because God is faithful, God gives us what we need. But because we are idiots, we don't always know what we really need. God certainly allows us to pray for what we *think* we need—including parking spaces and sunshine on one's wedding day. But God reserves the right to give us what we *actually* need—even if it's the last thing we *want*. That's God's way of rescuing us from self-deception and self-satisfaction. This rescue is called "salvation"—the radical reordering of our wants. (See Q. 1). It often hurts. But then again, we can't bear eternity (see Q. 2) unless our wants are purified, unless we learn to want only what is truly worth having.

4. *What is the difference between a "blessing" and "salvation"?* St. Catherine of Sienna once said, "All the way to heaven *is* heaven." (I suppose one could say the same about hell; see Q. 2.) Blessings are the individual steps on the long road to salvation: they are God's way of leading us forward, one step at a time. Of course, part of what it means to know that one is "saved" is to know how to construe all events and experiences—including those which hurt (see Q. 3) as "blessings." But I see, upon rereading your question, that you are referring specifically to the "blessings" mentioned in Jesus' Beatitudes. That doesn't change my answer, however. Poverty, sorrow, persecution—these things teach us self-detachment, i.e., salvation. Hungering and thirsting (especially "after righteousness") and being a peacemaker—

these are things that constitute the blessedness of the self-detached, the actions and attitudes of those who are "on the way" to heaven (and are therefore already "in" heaven).

5. *Is our conception of having a "personal relationship with Jesus Christ" actually biblical, etc.?* Yes . . . and no. Everything hinges on what we mean by "personal." If it is used as a synonym for "private," and carries connotations of chumminess, sentimentality, and exclusivity, I would say no. If it is used as a synonym for a corporate reality that includes *all of us* in the church, and *the whole of each of us* (including, therefore our characteristics as social beings), I would say yes. Put more concretely, I would say that Jesus is like the head of a huge family: everyone "knows" and "loves" him, but that knowledge and love is finally inseparable from the knowledge and love we have for everyone else in the family. Each of us has free and unrestricted access to him; but none of us "has him all to himself."

6. *What is Jesus talking about when he refers to the Kingdom of God/Heaven?* Himself. Origen of Alexandria was right when he said that Jesus is the *autobasilea*, that is, "the kingdom in person." The kingdom of God is the event of divine self-disclosure, which occurs whenever anyone forgives a sin or accepts forgiveness—"for Jesus' sake," whenever anyone rights a wrong or acknowledges being in the wrong—"for Jesus' sake," whenever anyone feeds the hungry, clothes the naked, heals the sick, visits the prisoner, or preaches good news to the poor—"for Jesus' sake." This is much more than a pious platitude, however, because genuine reconciliation to God means really feeling the bite of guilt; genuine service to the hungry means knowing what it's like to have an empty belly; genuine attention to the imprisoned requires that we know loneliness from personal experience; and preaching

effectively to the poor means being *with* the poor in their poverty.

7. *Which does God honor more—someone who earnestly struggles and seeks and wants to have faith, but ultimately rejects it? Or someone who blindly accepts a "faith," and never questions?* Remember what Aslan says in the Narnia Chronicles: "I tell no one any story but his own." That is, I don't think we *can* know, and I don't think it's safe to assume that we *could* know, who God honors "more" than whom. Personally, I'm inclined to believe that God ultimately embraces all who truly seek him, even if, in this life, they do not seem to find him. (That does not mean, however, that I regard doubt *per se* as a virtue.) And I'm also inclined to believe that God ultimately embraces all who know him in the simplicity of their hearts, even if, in this life, they have not thought too deeply about matters theological. (That does not mean, however, that I equate spiritual simplicity with religious stupidity.)

Well, those are my brief answers to your very profound and complex questions, as best as I can do on short notice and late at night. I look forward to talking them over with you at greater length in the months ahead.

Warm regards,

RBS

NOTES

1 Repeated attempts to contact this student for permission to include his letter in this volume were unsuccessful. But as with the authors of all the letters published here, his name has been changed in order to protect his privacy.

2 According to its website, Awana is an international, Bible-centered children's and youth ministry providing local churches with weekly clubs, programs and training for students in preschool through high school. <http://www.awana.org/>, September 14, 2005.

3 At SPU, every dormitory floor has a Student Ministry Coordinator (SMC) who is responsible for the spiritual life of the residents. He or she organizes Bible studies, prayer groups, accountability groups, retreats, etc. The SMC works closely with the Peer Advisor, who is responsible for upholding the university's lifestyle standards, organizes social activities, offers peer counseling, manages interpersonal conflicts, and generally keeps order.

CHAPTER 2

READING
SCRIPTURE
WITH NEW EYES

Close one eye. When you look out onto the world, it seems flattened, two-dimensional. Individual things are still *there*, and you can see them clearly enough one by one. But the spatial relations among them are hard to pick out. Walk around, and you may bump into things. Now open your eye again. Your depth perception returns. You can see how things are positioned with respect to each other. This is called stereoscopic vision.

We need to read the Bible stereoscopically, too. It's not enough to look *at* it: we need to look *into* it. It's not enough to read individual verses one by one, even if we do so with the greatest reverence and respect. We must read each passage in its immediate literary context and in relation to the Bible's overall message. To see the Bible in its depth, and as a whole, we need to study it from two different angles of vision at once. Only then can we can see it for what it truly is. First, we must read the Bible as the Word of God for the people of God. It is filled with judgments, challenges, commandments, invitations, and promises. These are addressed not just to the characters in the text, or to the original readers of the text, but also to us. Second, we must read the Bible as a diverse collection of time-bound, culture-conditioned, and artistically crafted human writings, each of which was composed in a specific social and historical context (which sometimes can be partially reconstructed by scholars), and each of which reflects the stylistic tastes, compositional conventions, and religious convictions of its original author and audience.

What happens if we read the Bible *only* as the Word of God, and pay no attention to its human elements, i.e., to the historical, social, cultural, literary, and religious character of these ancient documents? In our efforts to respect its "truthfulness," we may feel an impulse to assert its "inerrancy." In our attempt to honor the Bible's saving message, we may start to venerate its very words as sacred oracles, as if its spiritual validity and moral authority depended on the absolute accuracy and internal consistency of the text as it stands. This view leads us into absurdities. Consider just one. According to Matthew 27:5, Judas hanged himself. According to Acts 1:18, he was disemboweled. Now a man can't die twice and in two different ways. But does that mean we must figure out some way to "reconcile" these drastically discrepant accounts—say, by suggesting that after he hanged himself the rope broke and he fell headlong on a sharp rock? That would suggest that the Holy Spirit had suppressed part of a terrific story, only to assign us the task of defending the Bible's validity by concocting an implausible hypothesis. Clearly, this approach to Scripture won't do.

But what if we read the Bible only as a collection of ancient documents, the fragmentary record of long-dead people? Well, we are no longer saddled with the need to "prove" the accuracy of these documents or to harmonize their sometimes discrepant testimonies. We can read the texts on their own terms and in light of what we know about when, how, why, and by whom they were originally written. We can read them as great religious literature, as a treasure-trove of spiritual insights, moral values, and practical wisdom from our ancestors. So if there are two different accounts of Judas's death, maybe that's because the exact details of the story reflect the different literary-theological objectives of Matthew and Luke. There's surely a gain here. But what does this approach do for our conviction that the Bible has continuing relevance and binding authority? Are we to honor only those parts of it that we happen to *like*? Or worse, are we to regard the whole thing merely as the subject of antiquarian curiosity, but not as the source of divine revelation? Something is missing here, too.

Each of these ways of reading the Bible, taken by itself, flattens the text, the one by suppressing its literary complexity and beauty, the other by draining it of its revelatory power. But both of these ways of reading the Bible, taken together, enable us to see its true depth, its paradoxical nature as the Word of God conveyed in the words of God's faithful servants. Looking at the Bible stereoscopically enables us to hear "what the Spirit is saying to the churches" (Revelation 2:7) *through* the sacred text without being straitjacketed by a deadening literalism (cf. 2 Corinthians 3:6). This isn't the place to discuss the various proposals that have been made for exactly *how* this double-angled approach to the Bible is to be carried out.[1] It is enough to note here that this approach rescues us from the kind of piety that closes its eyes to historical-critical scholarship, and from the kind of scholarship that ignores the Bible's well-attested affective appeal and morally transformative power. Put another way, this approach lets us affirm that the Bible is both inspired and inspiring without having to prove that it is errorless; and it lets us affirm that the Bible is both the product and the possession of a historical community without having to deny that it is the preeminent medium of divine grace.

SUBJECT: THE BIBLE AND CHRISTIAN
         DOCTRINE

Dr. Steele,

Thank you for your time yesterday. You gave me a lot of useful information. However, I still have a few questions. You explained to me that the Bible is a tool with imperfect information in it, unless you read it in context. I understand that, but I don't understand why people constantly use one verse to form doctrine that easily could have been nonfactual just like the animal in Leviticus that chews the cud.[2]

For example, Romans 10:9 says, "If you confess with your lips that Jesus is Lord and believe in your heart that God raised him from the dead, you will be saved." Now, I have doubts about the Trinity. It's not that I don't believe that Jesus Christ existed, I just have doubts about him being God. How do I know he wasn't just an amazing follower of God, so that God gave him super-human power? I didn't live to see his miracles! Anyways, because I am cynical, and I doubt, according to this verse, I am going to hell. All because I'm being thoughtful and logical. That doesn't seem fair to me.

So I guess, what I'm trying to say is, I'm sick of using the Bible as a dictionary for Christian doctrine, when we don't really know what is factual and non-factual information about God. I try to read the Bible purely as a reference of somebody's trials and tribulations with God, and take these stories into account of my life. And when somebody in the Bible tells me that I'm going to hell because I have doubts about the Trinity, I will not take it as "truth" but "thought." Paul, in my mind, would be just like the people of today having their own thoughts about God, but not necessarily having the truth. Yes, Paul was an amazing believer, but he is still not perfect, just like the author of Leviticus. In my opinion, I think if the Puritans and the Christians during slavery times would have looked at the Bible as more of a story book rather than a book that can justify just about anything, then the movement in their faith would have been more successful and logical.

Is this wrong to think like this? Please be as critical as possible! I am seeking the "truth," and I think before I move on with my relationship with God, I need a little bit more logic. It makes it easier for me to map out my thoughts. Thank you so much for your insight!

Colin

Dear Colin:

1. I would not use the expression, "the Bible is a tool with imperfect information in it." That statement seems to presuppose at least three things that I would question: (a) that we are in a position to determine what "perfect information" would look like, (b) that the purpose of any book must be to convey "information" of some type, and (c) that the purpose of the Bible must be to convey "information" about God. I would prefer to say that, among many other things, the Bible is a testimony to what its authors (and the religious communities to which and for which they spoke) believed God had done in the world, in human history (and particularly in the history of the people of Israel and of the early Christian church), and in their own lives. A testimony is more than raw, objective "information." It reflects the point of view of the one who gives it. That does not make it false, but it does mean that it is shaped by a definite perspective. This perspective includes the life situation of the person making the testimony, i.e., the social, economic, political, and religious contexts in which he or she lived. It also reflects the way in which the person believes his or her own life has been changed by what he or she takes to be the work of God to which s/he is attesting. Thus, it is better to say that the Bible is a book of witness rather than a book of information.

2. At the moment I am at home, sitting at my wife's computer in her "office," which is really our laundry room. Beside me are two brand new appliances, a Maytag washer and dryer. Marilyn bought them after careful research into the pros and cons of various models. She got information, as one does when one is making decisions about *things*. But when one is making decisions about *persons*, one needs more than information. You don't marry a person on the basis of her height, weight, and eye color. True, you would make a sort of "background check" in the course of dating her. That is, you would find out about her past. But your purpose would not be merely to know whether she has all the "features" you want in "the perfect wife." That approach would be unspeakably crass—as if the suitability of a person could be ascertained through a punch list. No, your purpose would be to know *her* as a person. And that is both more and less than knowing information about her. So, too, with the Bible's testimony to God. It does, of course, tell you that God did this and that. But it does so because it wants to affirm who God is, what God wants, how God stands related to us. And it does so because it wants to invite you, its reader, into a living faith with that God. That is, it wants you to share the living faith of its human authors, which is itself a gift of its Divine Author, the Holy Spirit.

3. Living faith is a "personal relationship" with God, as we evangelicals say. It is trust in God. Like all relationships, it has its ups and downs, must grow over time or stagnate and die, and must weather all sorts of "tests." Like any friend, the God attested to in the Bible is not afraid of being asked hard questions about his purposes and reasons for doing this or that. But God doesn't always answer such questions directly. Often he "answers" our questions by posing questions of his own to us or by sending us to do things in his service.

We learn the "truth" about God, not by playing a game of Twenty Questions with him, but by patiently, faithfully living in his company and doing his bidding. "Answers" to our questions do come as time goes by, as the relationship deepens. Sometimes our questions themselves simply drop away. When my daughter was diagnosed with a dreadful, incurable illness, I asked God, "Why?" God never answered that question directly. I don't expect he ever will. In a sense, I hope he doesn't. For I have learned that what matters is not "why" Sarah is afflicted with this illness, but what marvelous things God is doing in her life, and my life, and the lives of our family and friends and neighbors through her suffering. What God is doing *through* Sarah doesn't "justify" what her screwed-up genes are doing *to* her. Intellectually, I would be dissatisfied, and morally I would be outraged, by any such attempts at justification. But in faith I have discovered deep meaning in her sufferings.[3]

4. How does this pertain to you? Perhaps in this way: A person who sincerely wants to know the truth about God is on a holy quest. I believe that God honors such quests, and is exceedingly patient with anyone who, in the course of his or her quest, raises questions about such puzzling theological truth claims as the deity of Christ or the triune nature of God. Personally, I believe that the classical, orthodox "answers" to such questions are faithful to the testimony of Scripture, confirmed by the corporate experience of the church and my own personal experience, and warranted by such rational assessment as we finite, fallible human beings can make about the mysteries of God. Indeed, I believe I have been called by God to spend my life explaining such "answers" to students. But I also believe that a person's quest for the "truth about God" consists in something much more than having answers to big questions. It means making a leap of faith.

It means surrendering joyfully to the Holy Mystery, which is beyond questions and answers, submitting obediently to God's will as it is revealed in the Bible. It means entering into that relationship in which our questions to God often get "answered" when God starts asking nosy questions of us, or when God sends us on "missions" to do things on his behalf for other people.

5. So, Colin, by all means ask your big theological questions. Don't get too bent out of shape by people who tell you that you are going to hell because you don't have a perfectly orthodox view of the Blessed Trinity. (And by the way, the Bible itself doesn't say that, whatever some of its well-meaning but severely misguided defenders may think!) The main thing is not to fool yourself into thinking that the search for a meaningful faith consists only in finding convincing answers to puzzling questions. It consists partly in that, but only partly, and as I have said, sometimes the seemingly puzzling questions aroused by our intellectual curiosity or existential predicament simply fall away. But the real search is a search for God Himself, not for a satisfying theology, and the "saving faith" you desire comes when you learn to listen to the "still, small voice" within you, when you learn to let Scripture question you (rather than vice versa), and when you learn that obedience and worship are not the result of success in your quest, but rather the preconditions for success in that quest.

6. As far as your specific questions on the doctrines of the person of Christ and of the Holy Spirit, let me speak exceedingly briefly. (You will need to take a course or two in systematic theology to understand the rationale for all I am about to say.) As far as the deity of Christ goes, there are only one or two passages (in the Gospel of John and

the Letter to the Colossians) where Christ is specifically said to be "God." There are many other places in the New Testament, of course, where Jesus is said to be "Christ" (a Greek translation of the Hebrew word "Messiah," meaning the Anointed One, i.e., the one designated with divine authority to rule God's people on earth) or "Son of God" (a common Hebrew term that did itself not always imply virginal conception or incarnation) or "Lord" (a term used in the Old Testament primarily of God). But there is a notable development of christological (and trinitarian) doctrine over the first five centuries of Christian history. And although the New Testament is at the root of that development, and clearly established the lines of thinking that were to come to full flower in the period of the ecumenical councils, it cannot be said that the New Testament clearly and consistently regards Jesus Christ as "God" in the sense that came to have in the Nicene Creed (AD 325; rev. AD 381) or the Chalcedonian Formula (AD 451). Yet the New Testament clearly does regard Jesus as the proper object of worship and of obedience. And as the Fathers of the Church argued, he cannot be the object of worship and obedience unless he is God. Still, whatever it means to affirm the deity of Jesus, the New Testament and the Fathers alike realized that it cannot mean that he is somehow less than or other than fully and truly human. Thus, his deity must be manifest in his humanity, not in spite of it. But as one penetrates ever more closely in faith and obedience into his human person, one comes to see that there is something uniquely authoritative, uniquely salvific, and uniquely worthy of adoration about this man. He is, in short the God-Man.

7. And if Jesus is the God-Man, then one is forced to revise one's understanding of God. One cannot affirm polytheism without denying the fundamental religious insight of the Old

Testament, and one cannot deny the fundamental religious insight of the Old Testament without making the New Testament completely unintelligible in other ways. Thus, one cannot deny Hebrew monotheism, even when one wants to affirm the deity of Jesus Christ and even when one wants to affirm the distinction between the Father and the Son. When you proceed down that road, and then factor in as well the "personal" presence of the Holy Spirit in the lives of the faithful, you are heading straight for the doctrine of the Trinity. But again, the New Testament never uses the word "Trinity," and affirms the "doctrine" of the Trinity only embryonically and implicitly. The fully articulated doctrine does not emerge until the Councils of Nicea (AD 325) and Constantinople (AD 381).

Yours,

RBS

SUBJECT: SCRAMBLED

Dear Dr. Steele:

Okay, you said whenever we get to the point of being so confused that our faith is at stake to speak up, so here I am, once again.

I have been thinking about our discussion about the story of Adam and Eve being myth in the way we defined it. Then, the other day I decided to read Job. As I was reading the section where God and Satan are conversing about allowing temptations and torture to be brought upon Job to prove he would either fail God or faithfully stand strong for God, no matter what awful things happened to him, I couldn't help but think, "There was no one to write that conversation down, how did they come up with that?" Now I am starting to wonder how many places like that in the stories in the Bible will cause me to be skeptical of the truth. But at the same time there is so much more that has had witnesses that it does not seem like it should be that big of an issue for me. It is not like I myself have not experienced the wonders of God without having a specific conversation with him that I could quote. I know there is so much more proof than straight word of mouth. It is just hard not to be skeptical at times.

Confused

Dear "Confused,"

I can't help but chuckle a bit by the subject heading of your post: "scrambled." The first time I tried to access your post, my entire computer got "scrambled." It locked up and somehow logged off the Internet server. After a bit of putzing, I managed to get back on-line, but I was very wary about trying a second time to access your post. Now, having read it, I'm wondering if this was some sort of divine retribution for the crisis of faith I seem to have precipitated!

Seriously, I thank you for speaking up about your "confusion," and I certainly want to be sure that this course does not jeopardize your faith. So here goes at least a partial reply to your query: What you have encountered through your study of theology and your own reading of Scripture is something that *every* theologically informed modern reader of the Bible encounters at some point or other. And that is the question of what it can mean to affirm the inspiration of Scripture once we acknowledge a seemingly inescapable fact about the text, namely that it reflects the social, political, and cultural situation of its human authors, as well as their religious views and literary tastes and styles. There are, or course, models of Scripture which assert that the text is simply a divine stenographic exercise, i.e., that God simply dictated what he wanted in the Bible to the human authors. Of course, on such models the human "authors" were really just secretaries, who simply copied down what God told them, word for word. But that model has its own serious problems—many of them, in fact, but the worst of which is that it seems to make the Bible more "holy" than Jesus himself. For it has the effect of denaturing or dehumanizing the Scriptures: they become "fully divine," but cease any longer to be "fully human." In effect—and after yesterday's lecture, I can now use this term with you—the verbal dictation theory of Scripture is really a kind of hermeneutical monophysitism.[4]

But if we are going to be dyophysites in our Christology (Jesus is one Person in two Natures), must we not also be dyophysites in our hermeneutics? Presumably so. But if we grant that the Bible has "human elements," we have to face quite seriously the kinds of problems that you have discovered, that whatever its message may be, it comes packaged in literary forms that have their own stylistic and compositional conventions, and involves religious ideas that develop over time, and reflects the ways that different people (dozens of them!) at different times (over an 1100-year time-span!) in different places (from as far east as Babylon to as far west as Rome!) lived and thought and prayed and sinned and struggled. At first, that thought can be very scary. It might seem to make the Bible less trustworthy as a witness to God's truth. But consider: if the Holy Spirit is faithfully and persistently at work among the people of God, as we have every reason to believe, then doesn't the very multiplicity of voices which speak to us from the pages of Scripture actually imply a *greater* reliability, a *deeper* truthfulness, a *wider* range and scope of witness, and a *closer* attention to human need and human experience than a book whose authors were mindless automatons, human tape recorders? What we must see is that the Holy Spirit works *through* people, not just *upon* them; that divine truth is *embodied* in the grand conversation that God's children have been having with God and with each other over the generations, and not just *piped* into us from some kind of heavenly data bank.

Let me make this more concrete: The prologue of Job tells us about a conversation "in heaven" between God and Satan. Satan? In heaven? What's he doing there? Why does God question him about his coming and goings? Doesn't God know? And why does he receive permission to do very nasty things to Job? Just for the purpose of proving Job's faithfulness? Can all this be taken absolutely literally? Well, yes. But if so, the picture of God that emerges is far more theologically problematic than it would be if we simply said that this conversation in heaven is really a literary contrivance that serves to frame the conversation, which takes place on earth between Job and his friends. It thus establishes the divine backdrop against which the puzzling mysteries and agonizing realities of earthly life are lived. And doesn't that way of looking at the text of Scripture make it feel *more* inspired—and more inspiring—than the kind of literalism that raises all those picayune and unanswerable questions itemized at the beginning of this paragraph?

Best,

RBS

SUBJECT: FAITH: PERSONAL OR COMMUNAL?

Dr. Steele,

I have several questions that need clarification about today's lecture. My first question regards "devotionalism." The point was brought up that faith is not personal, but community-wide. The design of salvation is to bring other people to know God. While I agree with this I also feel that salvation and faith are very personal. While the goal of every person should be to bring other souls to God, no one would or could give up their own "personal" salvation for any number of people. Salvation is a person's most treasured gift. It is given to each one of us by God—personally. Being saved is having a "personal" relationship with God. The Bible states that all heaven rejoices when one soul finds the Lord. Not a community.

My second question is the last section we talked about in class. Migliore says that "Scripture must be interpreted with the help of literary and historical criticism; yet scripture's unique witness to God resists its reduction to pious fiction or its imprisonment in the past"[5] and that in the end, the Bible is God's word. I feel that Migliore is talking out both sides of his mouth. He states that biblicism—the belief that the Bible is dictated and therefore inerrant is dangerous, yet at the same time that the Bible is God's word. God's word is inerrant. Second, he states that the Bible is not historically accurate and yet that it is a "unique witness to God." Are not the creation, the great flood, the parting of the red sea, etc., testimonies to God's great power? God needs no embellishment of tales, and I'm sure the apostles knew this.

If we disregard part of the Bible—for example, the creation—as a "lovely story," its still greater claims come into question. The persecution, crucifixion, and resurrection of Jesus Christ is a phenomenal account that far surpasses any in the world. I would hate to think the foundations of my faith are just a "lovely story" someone wrote.

Leslie

Dear Leslie,

Regarding devotionalism, if I understand your question correctly, I think you may be working with a false dichotomy. To say that faith is the common "possession of" (or, as you are quite right to say, "gift to") the Christian community is not to deny that it is deeply "personal." It is only to deny that it is something that individuals can "possess" by and for themselves. We only come into full personhood through participation in community, and into full personhood in Christ through participation in Christ's family. One does not first have a "personal relationship with Christ" and then decide to participate in the life of the church, for one cannot get into a "personal relationship with Christ" except through the ministry of the church. Even somebody converted to Christ by reading a Gideon Bible all alone late at night in a motel room does so as the beneficiary of the church's ministry. For the very existence of the Bible, its passing-down from generation to generation through the centuries, its placement in the motel room all presuppose the existence of a faith community which names the Bible as its Scripture.

As to your second question, the doctrine that the Scriptures are inspired, i.e., that they are (or convey) the Word of God for the people of God must always be distinguished from any particular theory of how this is so. To reject the theory of inerrancy is not to reject the doctrine of the inspiration of Scripture; it is only to reject one way of thinking about how that inspiration comes to be. Similarly, the validity of the Scripture's witness to God's power in creation does not depend on the "historical accuracy" of Genesis 1–3. For the very point of the creation narratives is to make, not a *scientific* claim as to how long it took God to make the universe, but rather a *theological* claim that it was Yahweh (and not, for example, blind fate or one of the other deities, such as those in the pantheons of the Canaanites, the Mesopotamians, or the Egyptians) who was "the maker of heaven and earth."

I hope this clarifies matters.

RBS

SUBJECT: DOES THE BIBLE HAVE ERRORS?

Dr. Steele,

I didn't fully understand what you were saying about the fundamentalist view of the Bible. This could be totally wrong, but it sounded like you were saying that the Bible is the inspired work of God written through imperfect human hands. It almost sounded like you were saying that because it was written by humans that we have to take it as such and watch for errors. You never came out and said it, but it felt like you were on the verge of saying such. I don't think you were making a claim that the Bible has errors, but what exactly were you saying? Were you just reminding us that the Bible needs to be read in light of the style and the culture it was written in, or what?

Thank you,

Jack

Dear Jack:

Let me clarify my comments about the "hermeneutical docetism" of fundamentalists. They were perhaps a bit extravagant and overly general, and if so, I am willing to be taken out to the woodshed. I was simply referring to the fact that in the name of protecting the divine authority of Scripture some people actually do it a grievous disservice by implying that it somehow dropped fully formed from heaven, that its every verse is immediately perspicuous to every sincere believer, that its contents are self-interpreting, that it possesses a single, univocal, and absolute "meaning," and that no attention needs to be paid by contemporary readers to the historical, social and religious context in which its various books were written. Such people believe that because the Bible is a "holy book," it must be wholly free from any of the things that go into the composition of other books and into the compiling of libraries, and that its interpretation is a simple matter of endlessly restating its obvious, literal meaning. All of those notions are plainly false. In one sense, therefore, I guess I *was* saying that the Bible was written by "imperfect human hands."

But that doesn't mean that the Word of God is somehow "imperfect." It only means that the Word of God must not simply be identified with the text of Scripture. Indeed, Scripture itself asserts that the Word of God was *incarnate* in Jesus Christ: he alone is perfect. And although he preached a message, and lived what he preached, he wrote nothing. The content of his message and the story of his life, death, and resurrection were *preached* by prophets and apostles and *recorded* by evangelists. They were human beings whom God used for the purpose of proclaiming the incarnate and risen Word, Jesus Christ himself. And thus their words are said to "be" the Word of God—meaning, however, that they are the normative form in which the gospel of Christ is transmitted. In other words, the Word of God is "contained" and "conveyed" in the words of human beings—and the human qualities of the "container" (literary form, historical context, etc.) must be acknowledged and accounted for if we are rightly to interpret the contents for the people of God.

RBS

NOTES

1 The literature on this subject is enormous. Some useful overviews include: Raymond E. Brown, *Biblical Exegesis and Church Doctrine* (New York and Mahwah, NJ: Paulist Press, 1985); Brevard S. Childs, *Biblical Theology of the Old and New Testaments* (London: SCM/Minneapolis: Fortress, 1992); John Goldingay, *Models for Scripture* (Grand Rapids: Eerdmans Publishing Co. & Carlisle: Paternoster Press, 1994); Van Harvey, *The Historian and the Believer* (New York: Macmillan, 1966); David H. Kelsey, *The Uses of Scripture in Recent Theology* (Philadelphia: Fortress Press, 1975); Sandra M. Schneiders, *The Revelatory Text* (Collegeville, MN: Liturgical Press, 1999).

2 One of my most challenging tasks as a teacher of theology at a Christian university, where so many students have inerrantist views of Scripture, is to show that the theological truthfulness of the Bible doesn't depend on the "facticity" of every statement it makes or seems to make—where the criterion of facticity is "scientific accuracy." One of my typical ways of arguing that this claim, however well-meant, is untenable, is to appeal to Leviticus 11:2–8, where the Israelites are prohibited from eating rock badgers and rabbits, because they "chew the cud but do not part the hoof." Now, neither of these animals is classified today as a ruminant, even though their eating habits might have some superficial resemblances to those of cows, camels, sheep, etc. Thus something the Bible presumes clearly contradicts something we know on scientific grounds. I like to use this example in class, because even the most stridently literalistic students are already prone to discount the theological significance of the Old Testament kosher laws, and are thus less scandalized than they typically are if the teacher challenges, say, the cosmology of Genesis 1–3. Of course, that fact itself is very instructive, because it reveals that despite their commitment to the plenary inspiration of Scripture, in practice they still regard some parts of the Bible as more sacred, or at least more deserving of rigorous defense, than others.

3 Those interested in Sarah's condition and in my reflections on raising a child with serious disabilities, see "Accessibility or Hospitality?" *The University of Pennsylvania Orthopaedic Journal*, 9 (Spring 1993): 45–51; and "Unremitting Compassion: The Moral Psychology of Parenting Children with Genetic Disorders." *Theology Today* 57:2 (July 2000): 161–174.

4 Monophysitism (lit. "one-nature-ism") was a school of theology that emerged in the wake of the Council of Ephesus (AD 431). It teaches that human nature was not only "assumed" by the Son of God at the moment of incarnation (as the orthodox Cappadocian Fathers had taught), but was "absorbed by," "confused with," or "changed into" the divine nature, and thus essentially obliterated by it. This view was condemned at the Council of Chalcedon (AD 451) because it dehumanizes Jesus and renders him incapable of being humanity's savior.

5 Daniel L. Migliore, *Faith Seeking Understanding: An Introduction to Christian Theology* (Grand Rapids: Eerdmans Publishing Co, 1991), 49. I used this book for some years as a text in my course, "Introduction to Christian Theology."

CHAPTER 3

WHO DO WE SAY THAT CHRIST IS?

The story goes that when Jesus and his disciples were touring the district of Caesarea Philippi, he put a question to them: "Who do people say that I am?" Apparently he was aware of the buzz that his ministry had created and knew that they were aware of it, too. They answered that opinions were divided. Some said he was Elijah back from heaven, or John the Baptist back from the dead, or another of the ancient prophets. Then he asked them a much harder question: "But who do *you* say that I am?" (Mark 8:22–33; Matthew 16:13–23; Luke 9:18–22, emphasis added).

With the first question, Jesus may be said to have invented "Christology," the branch of Christian theology devoted to comparing, contrasting, analyzing, and critiquing various views of who he is. With the second question, Jesus exposed an error into which Christology is in constant danger of falling, namely the error of supposing that it is sufficient to offer an inventory of other people's views. Christology can never be an armchair discipline; it is inevitably personal—or it falsifies the very data with which it works. Jesus can never merely be the object of dispassionate study; he insists on being the object of devotion. To study what others have said about Jesus without asking who *I* myself say that he is, who he is *for me*, is to mistake the whole point.

To prevent my classes and myself from making this mistake, I like to reverse the order of the two questions that Jesus asked his disciples. That is, instead of beginning with a survey of other people's views, I ask them to write a brief statement of their own. Many of them use the Christological titles found in the New Testament ("Son of God," "Savior," etc.). Others invent their own formulas, which are sometimes of great power and beauty.[1] As we study the history of the doctrines of the person and work of Christ from the New Testament to modern times, I have the students rewrite their first paper in light of what they have been learning. Throughout the course we keep revisiting the existential question, "Who do *I* say that he is?"

My own Christological views are fairly orthodox. I share the classical Christian conviction that the New Testament witness to who Jesus was and what he did during his earthly ministry presumes that he stood, and eternally stands, in a unique filial relationship with the Father; that he embodied the Father's infinite and absolute love for all humanity; that he transmits it, via his Spirit, to those who humbly place their trust in him and obediently pattern their lives according to his example; and that none of these things can ever rightly be said of anyone else, however much respect we may want to accord to, and however much moral wisdom and religious insight we may be able to glean from, any of the other saints, sages, seers, prophets, martyrs, and heroes who have graced human history. The uniqueness and perfection of Jesus' divine/human nature and the decisiveness and finality of his saving work on behalf of the human race are the fundamental premises of the New Testament, taken as a whole, and are the foundation of the historic Christian faith, in all its diverse institutional expressions and cultural manifestations.

SUBJECT: IS CHRISTIANITY THE "CULT OF JESUS"?

Hi Dr. Steele,

I have been thinking a lot about the subject of this class and trying to understand how Christ ought to figure into my life and in what ways. Dr. Lemcio said in my New Testament class last year that "Christianity is not a cult of Jesus." I appreciated that so much, given the way I feel about all the Jesus talk I hear on this campus and from Christians in general. In no way do I want to deny the profound significance of Christ's existence, but even Jesus always turned the attention back to the Father. Those who believe in him believe not in him but in him who sent him (Mark 12:45, I think). And so it frustrates me that I have grown up singing most of the songs in church to Jesus and always praying to Jesus. But isn't it true that Jesus isn't the object, but the Father who sent Jesus? I don't understand because at the same time I am saying this I affirm the Christian faith, the center of which is Jesus Christ. I desire to worship God in a way that is the most respectful to God, and it concerns me that the focus on God as a whole may be lost in the emphasis on Jesus. I notice people often using terms like "God" and "Jesus" all as interchangeable, but ought they be? I wonder if all the Jesus talk, which has become trite, leaves people with a very shallow understanding of what being like Christ really means for us. My criticism of Christians' sole emphasis on Jesus is not out of disrespect, but out of a call to have more respect. I am not convinced that gathering together 200 people in Brougham (I don't mean to gang up on Group, I'm merely using it as an example) to sing songs about Jesus that probably only a fraction of them really understand is the most respectful way to worship God.[2] I wish I wasn't so judgmental, but to stifle what I think and to go on never bringing up the concerns I have would only mean that I could not be sincere, then, in worship, prayer, conversation, etc., about God. I guess I am just wondering if you have anything to say that may be helpful for me to understand. We'll talk sometime.

Thanks.

Rose

Dear Rose,

Thanks for you powerful and probing "thoughts." In response to your observations, I must say that I agree very much with almost all of what you say. You may recall the passage in Migliore's *Faith Seeking Understanding* where he cautions us against "the Unitarianism of the Second person of the Trinity,"[3] that is, the kind of christocentrism that goes to seed in what we might even call Jesus-olatry. There are many reasons that this sort of thing happens in Christianity, and particularly in late twentieth century American evangelicalism, but the end result is precisely the kind of sickeningly sweet, cloyingly precious, religious emotionalism that you describe. Authentic Christian faith is surely more than having a weekly spiritual orgasm at Group. (And I don't mean to gang up on Group either; I've only gone once, when I was the guest speaker, and had a wonderful time. Indeed, I was very moved by the religious zeal I observed, even if I myself am too old and crotchety to experience and display it the way young people do.) At the same time, our attempt to avoid the "Unitarianism of the Second Person" can lead us to another position that the Christian tradition has found equally unsatisfactory. This is the sort of subordinationist Christology that denies the full deity of Christ, depersonalizes him, and in effect "instrumentalizes" him, turning him into a kind of useful audio-visual aid for the Father. A robust trinitarianism seeks to tread the fine line between these two aberrations, acknowledging Jesus' deity without reducing Jesus to one's own personal "household god." This, in fact, is *exactly* what the next section of our class deals with: the christological and trinitarian controversies of the fourth and fifth centuries, in which the Church Fathers sought a dogmatic articulation of that "fine line." Stay tuned. . . .

Cheers,

RBS

SUBJECT: CHRIST, THE "FULLY HUMAN ONE"

Hi Dr. Steele!

As I was looking over my notes from class today regarding the discussion of "The Classical Affirmations about the Person and Work of Christ," a thought occurred to me. I wholeheartedly agreed with what Kim said in class, that Jesus has a unique closeness with God. Therefore, when Jesus is tempted, He resists such temptations by turning to God. I want to add to this comment. I also see that because of His faithfulness and loyalty to God, God uses Jesus, the "fully human" one, as the supreme example of what a "full human" should be. Because we are fallen creatures and separated from God by sin, however, we are unable to have that supreme potential of being "fully human." I'm skeptical about saying that just because of what we learn in the Bible about Jesus—that He was sent into this world and did the works of God—we humans should ever hope to be like him. I know that we will never be able to become "fully human," because of the fact that sin separates us from God. I guess that my comment also turned into the question of whether it is right for me to look at this "affirmation" in this perspective. I would really appreciate your insight!

Miriam

Dear Miriam:

If I understand your comment/question correctly, you are
not so worried about the fact that we described Jesus as
the "truly [or fully] human one," as you are about the fact
that we described Jesus' saving work as his power to make
us truly [or fully] human. For that might be taken to imply
that we could attain a level of righteousness equal to his,
in which case we presumably would no longer need him
to be our savior. If that is indeed what you were getting at
in your question, I can only say that it is a very important
christological/soteriological insight. Certainly we don't want to
say anything about our Savior that would make it look as if we
didn't need him to be our Savior!

But let me put your question another way. Would it be
correct to say that we need our sin as much as we need our
Savior, because without our sin we wouldn't need, or have, a
Savior? That seems wrong, too, since it seems to give sin an
importance equivalent in our lives to that of Christ. I think a
better way to think of this might go like this: Through Christ,
and only through Christ, human beings are brought toward
their true nature, that is, into a state of perfect communion
with our Creator and with each other. For our true nature—
from which we have "fallen"—is to be "participants in the
divine nature." Such participation is impossible on our own,
but it must be possible through the transforming power of the
Spirit of the Risen Christ. If it weren't possible, what would
"salvation" mean? So it's not a question of getting to a point
where we don't need Christ. Rather, it's a question of allowing
Christ to bring us to the point where we can fully enjoy and
serve God, as God made us to do and wants us to do.

But how shall we think of that "point"? In my opinion, we
should not think of it as a *fixed* point at all, a destination

that we eventually get to (say, in heaven) and where we stand still thereafter forever and ever. Rather, it is a *moving* point, a receding horizon, an eternal journey *to* the Father, *with* Christ, and *in* the Holy Spirit. Without Christ's constant companionship, without the Spirit's perpetual empowerment—beginning even now, but continuing forever in heaven—the journey to God would be impossible. And the journey can be described as growing *both* ever more fully and truly human *and* ever more fully and truly "spiritual" or "divine." For if being truly human is being fully open to the divine, that is, of being capable of genuine communion with the divine, and if divinity is inexhaustible, then being human is being fully open to the inexhaustible delights of knowing and loving God.

Hope this helps.

RBS

SUBJECT: WHY DID JESUS HAVE TO DIE?

Dr. Steele,

I have been thinking about our class discussion yesterday and especially about the question, "Why did Jesus have to become a man and die for our redemption?" Do you think it is valid to entertain the thought that he had to come but that maybe he didn't have to die? This creates a problem though, since then we wouldn't really know why he died. We certainly don't want to say that it was for nothing or that it was just because the Pharisees and Romans killed him. Is the forgiveness of sin conditioned upon death or upon obedience? Are we forgiven because Jesus died and the payment for sin is death, or because he obeyed God even to the point of death on the cross? Do you think the bigger problem that Anselm discusses is only a problem because we make it a problem, or does it have more substance than that?

Chuck

Dear Chuck,

As a general rule, I'm a bit skeptical about questions that come in the form, "Did such-and-such have to happen?" Certainly I have great sympathy with Anselm's efforts to show that what *did* happen *had* to happen, i.e., that there is a divine wisdom manifest in the events of "salvation history," or, to put it in different categories, that there is a providential ordering "in, with, and under" *all* events, and that the good and grand purposes of God are somehow accomplished through the particularities and actualities of human history. If that is so, then it is a bit odd to ask if something could have been otherwise, because all we know is that things were as they were—and that God worked savingly through them. Yet skepticism about counterfactuals shouldn't be absolutized either. That is, it would appear to compromise the freedom of God to say that God *couldn't* have done things differently, *couldn't* have accomplished his purposes through some different set of events. That seems to bind the Author to the script, rather than to interpret the script in terms of the stated intentions of the Author.

That said, it appears to me that a religion that did not hold that Jesus "died for our sins in accordance with the Scriptures" would be something other than classical Christianity. It might, for example, be something like Ebionitism or Abelardism, with Jesus serving as the sage or prophet who taught God's ways to humankind, but who did not serve God as the sacrificial Lamb. Put succinctly, such a view of the "atonement" turns the crucifixion of Jesus into an unfortunate mistake made by the Jewish and Roman authorities—perhaps an over-reaction on their part to his revolutionary teachings or his alarming popularity with the mob. But then the cross ceases to be essential to who he was and what he did, or rather, to who God is and what God did through him. On the other hand, we certainly don't want to suggest that Jesus' passion and death were simply staged to appease God through bloodletting—especially if God himself did the staging. That is little more than barbarism. Going to the cross has to have been an action which Jesus, *qua* human being and faithful Jew, freely chose in obedience to what he took to be God's will for him, an action that he couldn't have avoided without betraying what was obviously most precious to him, namely the advancement of God's kingdom, but at the same time that he couldn't have wanted to do without ceasing to be a healthy, life-loving person. Indeed, I suspect that the pathos of his utterance, "My God, my God, why have you forsaken me," springs, at least in part, from the fact that he felt, as bitterly as any person can feel, the ghastly strangeness of the fact that God was offering life and righteousness to all people through the judicial murder of one, and that God had placed the "success" of this scandalous strategy in the hands of the one person who could rightly have refused to be his agent and who didn't stand to benefit personally from it. *That*, it seems to me, is the "offense" of the cross—and no one was more "offended" than Jesus himself.

Yours,

RBS

SUBJECT: CONDESCENDING CHRISTIANS[4]

Dear Rick,

Thanks for the wonderful and thoughtful response with examples that I intend on reading. Regarding the "scandal of particularity" it's nice to see others have had the same questions I've had, not only in this time frame, but in past centuries as well. I nevertheless can't help but sense in your words a kind of double standard. I, on the one hand, felt my position legitimized. On the other hand, I generally feel from Christians who are open, a condescending attitude. And in spite of their wonderfully open statements, they nevertheless seem to harbor a limited acceptance of non-Christian belief, as if they thought there was only one truth and that Christians have it. I guess generally speaking what is of concern for me in most of the stated Christian doctrine is a tendency to apply human values, human emotions onto a universal God. As for myself, I do not presume in the least to be able to have any significant understanding of the nature of God.

I find myself coming back to my first email. That is, why should we believe that God would be incarnate once and once only in all human history? If I accept that God is incarnate in Jesus the Christ, then I also must be open to the possibility of God's choice to be incarnate in multitudes of personalities.

This has been written on the fly, so hopefully it makes sense. I will continue to reread your letter. Thank you very much and I look forward to our next communication.

Luke

Dear Luke,

I am pretty sure that the following response to your suggestions that we Christians operate according to "a kind of double standard" and in a "condescending" manner toward persons of other faiths will not satisfy you. Indeed, I suspect it will seem to you to exemplify precisely the same attitude from which it is intended to exonerate us. I am not particularly worried if that is so. For it appears to be inevitable that when Christians and non-Christians engage in theological discussions, they eventually reach a point of irreconcilability. That, of course, does not mean that subsequent conversations between them are impossible or futile. It just means that there is one point—the radical difference between what Christians say about Jesus Christ and what adherents of other faiths are prepared to say about their "founders"—that makes it impossible for Christians to avoid the charge of being condescending. Let me state that problem as clearly as possible, and then speak (condescendingly?) about how *your* position seems to *us*.

Most (though not all) religions trace themselves to some founder, whose religious vision or experience becomes normative for his followers: Moses for Judaism, Gautama for Buddhism, Mohammed for Islam, Baha'Ullah for the Bahai faith, etc. These founders are seen, in some sense, as mediators between humanity and (what shall we call it?) "the divine," "the transcendent," "the All," "the Real," etc. But as venerated as those founders are by their followers (and they do sometimes take on semi-divine or quasi-divine status), and as exemplary as their lives are deemed to be by their followers, there is almost always a clear distinction made between the mediator and that divine reality which he mediates. Thus, Jews would find the suggestion that Moses be worshipped as God appalling, a violation of the first and foremost of the very commandments that Moses gave to his followers on God's behalf. So, too, Buddhists would see in Siddhartha Gautama a perfect exemplification of that "Buddha nature" to which all people ought to aspire and can, under the right conditions, achieve. No doubt the place of Moses in Judaism differs from the place of Gautama in Buddhism; and there are certainly other radical differences in those two religions. But there is at least this agreement between Jews and Buddhists, namely that their founders point the way which others must follow, but are not themselves the way. They reveal the truth, but they are not themselves the truth.

It is just here that Christianity's claim about Jesus differs so radically—and causes Christians to seem to adherents of other faiths so "condescending." For Christianity asserts that Jesus *is* "the way, the truth, and the life," that Jesus is not simply a model for us to venerate and emulate, but is himself the proper object of our worship. And as earnestly as Christians may want to engage in constructive and respectful dialogue with adherents of other faiths, they cannot concede on this point, or place Jesus on the same level as Moses or Gautama or Mohammed (even if only for purposes of discussion) without denying the principle of their own faith. And to do *that*, to deny the first principle of their faith, would defeat the very purpose of engaging in inter-religious dialogue at all—namely, to explain their own position forthrightly to others, while at the same time listening attentively while others explain their position to them. Put differently, precisely because of the nature of the claims made by Christians about Christ, there is an irreducible aspect of *witness* that enters into every effort at *dialogue.*

Of course, this does not authorize Christians to be crass, self-congratulatory, or triumphalistic in their attitudes toward "non-Christians." (And I freely admit that the very word "non-Christian" upon Christian lips can have an unpleasantly smug ring to it!) Indeed, if Christians are true to their own claim about the kind of salvation that Christ brings to humanity, they must quite clearly understand themselves (as St. Paul did) as the "chief of sinners," that is, as people more in need of divine grace than anybody else—including people of other faiths! What could be humbler than that? On the other hand, they cannot in the name of religious egalitarianism deny the claim that makes them Christians in the first place—and that is the claim that the person whom they name as Savior is not just an instrument of God or a vehicle to God but is himself the one true incarnation of God.

But now let me pose a question to you. You state that you "do not presume in the least to be able to have any significant understanding of the nature of God." But if so, why do you assume that it would be more characteristic of God to incarnate himself more than once in human history? On what basis can you make such an assumption? Are you not, in fact, bootlegging an *a priori* theological assumption of your own into the conversation, and thereby suggesting that you *do*, in fact, have a "significant understanding of the nature of God," while claiming not to? And while you might be innocent of the charge that you have laid at my door (i.e., of being condescending), might you not be guilty of a certain inconsistency? For you apparently take yourself to have warrant for making claims about how God *would* or *should* act, while at the same time humbly professing ignorance on the matter.

Of course, I no more want to accuse you of being *intentionally* disingenuous (i.e., devious or dishonest) than I take you to be accusing me of being *crassly* condescending. I simply want to point out that there is no absolutely neutral starting point for theological discussions, and that all of us have certain presuppositions. And when we trace out what those presuppositions are, we find that some of them (not all) are non-negotiable and unrevisable. What happens when we get to that point is hard to predict.

Rick

NOTES

1 One student, addressing Christ directly, wrote: "You are both the Way and the Destiny. You are the center point of history and the vein of gold running through my life that will be revealed when You burn away the dross. You are at once Master and Servant, Shepherd and Lamb, Mercy and Justice, Water

and Rock, Peace and Sword, God and man." I would encourage you as you read this book or as you engage in your own study of theology to write a similar paragraph. You might find it very revealing.

2 "Group" is an informal, and usually very animated, student-led worship service held on Wednesday evenings. The service is led by a "praise band" (guitars, drums, electric keyboard, etc.) and the speakers usually address issues of keen personal interest to students.

3 Daniel L. Migliore, *Faith Seeking Understanding* (Grand Rapids: William B. Eerdmans Publishing Co., 1991), 65. I was quoting from memory here— and misquoted. Migliore's actual expression is "the unitarianism of the Redeemer."

4 Unlike most of the people whose letters to me are included in this volume, the author of this post was not my student. He is a middle-aged medical professional and was, at the time of this correspondence, dating a friend of mine from the Midwest. Their relationship was strained by the fact that she is a Christian minister, whereas he might best be described as a "seeker," one who is deeply interested in many of the great world religions, but committed to none of them. My friend had asked me to write to Luke to sketch out the Christian claim that in Jesus of Nazareth God is uniquely and decisively self-revealed to humanity. Regrettably, I did not save a copy of that letter, but as I recall, I tried to make as much allowance as possible for those elements of spiritual and moral truth in the other world religions which Christians can cheerfully acknowledge and gratefully learn from, while at the same time stoutly defending those twin non-negotiable Christian doctrines, Incarnation and Trinity.

CHAPTER 4

FREE CHOICE, MORAL RESPONSIBILITY, AND DIVINE SOVEREIGNTY

"The great debate" between Calvinism and Arminianism,[1] which began in Holland four centuries ago, and which caused grave divisions in the English and American churches during the seventeenth, eighteenth, and nineteenth centuries, still rages in evangelical circles today. I once spoke to a prospective student who belonged to a staunchly Calvinist church. He was worried about attending SPU, which is affiliated with the Free Methodist Church, whose doctrinal stance is Arminian, i.e., anti-Calvinist. Would his religious views be challenged and would his grades suffer if he refused to change his views? What is particularly instructive about the young man's questions is the assumption that underlies them, that to hold a religious conviction sincerely is to cordon it off from critical testing. It's not just that he wanted to find a college that would respect his beliefs. It's that he wanted to find a college that wouldn't challenge his beliefs. Or rather, it's that he assumed that professors who hold their beliefs as passionately as he held his would punish him for refusing to capitulate to them. I assured him that we didn't work that way. We wouldn't try to indoctrinate him, but we would try to educate him; we wouldn't penalize him for defending his views, but we would insist that he learn to take other views seriously. As we see it, being ready to make a "defense" of one's faith (cf. 1 Peter 3:15) means being willing to hear all sides of an argument. Responsible theology is patient dialogue.

This isn't the place to summarize Calvinism or Arminian-Wesleyanism. The literature on that subject is voluminous and readily available.[2] Moreover, many aspects of the controversy—predestination, free will, eternal security, human perfectibility, and so forth—are amply discussed in these letters. It is enough here to highlight the special challenge this controversy poses for me as a teacher. How can I be fair to both sides of an apparently irresolvable argument, and equally sensitive to the religious concerns of those who sit side by side in class but stand on opposite sides of the debate? I think two strategies are necessary.

First, we must all come to see that doctrinal disputes often can't be solved by citing Scripture, because each side has an arsenal of isolated proof texts at its disposal. The question is how are we to understand the *whole* of Scripture's witness. And that leads us to investigate the theological presuppositions that each of us *brings to* the Bible. We must realize that what we find in the Bible is often just what we've been taught to look for. That doesn't mean that what we find isn't really there. It means that more may be there than we expected to find.

Second, we must also learn that our theological presuppositions often reflect our emotional needs and socio-economic interests. Thus, learning why certain arguments seem persuasive to us, and why we interpret Scripture in a particular way, helps us become self-aware and self-critical. This can best be accomplished by asking why other people find other arguments persuasive, why they interpret Scripture differently. So, if a student asks herself *why* she finds Calvinism—with its doctrines of human depravity, predestination, limited atonement, and eternal security—so attractive, she might learn that it provides a way for her to deal with the frightful moral confusion, political turmoil, economic insecurity, and religious relativism of our world. She might learn that it helps her face the daunting responsibilities and alluring temptations of college life, the frightening precariousness of the job market, and her own restless and often frustrating quest for love. The doctrine of divine sovereignty is immensely consoling to one who is uncertain of her world and of herself. Conversely, if a student asks himself why he is persuaded by Arminian-Wesleyanism—with its stress on freedom of the will, moral responsibility, human perfectibility, and the all-inclusiveness of divine love—he might discover how deeply the ethos of egalitarianism and the myth of self-determination run in our national character. He learns to critique his belief that he is in control of his own destiny and that hard work and fair play are always rewarded in this world. To a bright, well-heeled collegian who cherishes the expectation of a happy marriage and a prosperous career, it is pleasant to think that the moral order of the universe corresponds to his interests.

I have no desire to rob dour-hearted Calvinists of their religious consolations or to disabuse earnest Arminians of their dreams. But we should understand that our spiritual and emotional needs predispose us to read the Bible *for* a certain message. Needless to say, the fact that we *want* something to be true doesn't *make* it true—or false. But knowing that we *want* something to be true can help us look more self-critically at our convictions and at how we weigh the evidence and arguments supporting those convictions. Put sharply, we can't assess the validity of our *reasons* for believing something until we know the *motives* that make us wish it to be true.

Students often ask me where I, myself, stand on the Calvinist/Arminian controversy. On the fence, I tell them, though tilting a bit toward the Arminian side. In fact, I believe that the deepest Christian wisdom comes from *refusing* to take too strong a stand on it, from leaving the question unanswered, at least "on paper." This isn't just because the biblical evidence is equivocal, or that pastoral experience teaches us that spiritual shipwreck may come from steering too close either to the Scylla of Calvinist presumption or the Charybdis of Arminian moralism. It's because I've come to realize that *my* motives shape the way I approach the question—and that my motives run in opposite directions. I *want* to believe in divine sovereignty; but I *also* want to believe in human responsibility. Why? Because the happiness I've experienced in life has always seemed to come to me as a divine gift, which I'm unworthy to enjoy. But that gift comes with a task, namely the duty to help others attain happiness, too. This paradox cannot be resolved "on paper," that is, on purely exegetical and dogmatic grounds. It can only be resolved in the living of the Christian life, where gratitude for undeserved mercies merges with a commitment to public service. The reconciliation of this paradox is existential, not intellectual.

SUBJECT: DIVINE ELECTION

Hey Dr. Steele,

I was reviewing Migliore's chapter on the Triune God.[3] In the section that talks about the electing grace of God, he states that God desires that everyone be saved. This has been a strong belief of mine, and so I do not question it. However, while I was reading the Gospel of Matthew in my devotions this morning, I came across some passages that seemed to contradict this point. In Matthew 10, when Jesus sends out the disciples, he commands them not to spread the gospel to the Gentiles or Samaritans. Later in the gospel, he even tried to send away the Canaanite woman because she was not Jewish. In Matthew 13, when the disciples came to Jesus and asked him why he spoke in parables, he quoted Isaiah and replied, "You will be ever hearing but never understanding; you will be ever seeing but never perceiving. For this people's heart has become calloused; and they hardly hear with their ears, and they have closed their eyes. Otherwise they might see with their eyes, hear with their ears, understand with their hearts and turn, and I would heal them" (Matthew 13:14–15). These words and actions seem to me to contradict the idea that Christ came for all to be saved. In fact, in the great commission, he commands us to bring the gospel to *all people*. How can these two totally different views fit together?

In Christ,

Lena

Dear Lena,

This is one of the thorniest and most controversial of all theological questions. Part of what drives the controversy is that the Bible itself seems to support *both* the more restrictive view that "the elect" are relatively small in number (144,000 according to Revelation 7:4), and that who they are is strictly predetermined "before the foundation of the world" (Ephesians 1:4–5), *and* the more "universalistic" view that "[God] desires everyone to be saved and to come to the knowledge of the truth" (1 Timothy 2:1–6). Texts for both positions could be multiplied, but I don't think the issue can finally be resolved by the method of "proof-texting." Where one stands on the issue—*if* one has to take a stand on it at all—will finally depend on one's understanding of God. Those who emphasize the majesty and sovereignty of God and the sinfulness of humanity generally opt for the idea of election (although many take the 144,000 number to be symbolic, rather than literal), while those who emphasize "the wideness of God's mercy" generally opt for the idea that "whosoever will, may come."

As a Wesleyan evangelical born and bred, I am committed to the more inclusive view. On the other hand, I have come to believe that whenever we find such apparent contradictions in the Bible, our response should not be to choose one position and discount the other, but rather to ask whether there is some important theological message that neither position alone can encompass. Or as I said in answer to another question, the "apparent contradictions" of the Bible are often real paradoxes, and what is lacking is a broader view that can enable you to see the elements of truth in both. And I think something like that is the case here. To put it simply and sharply, I would say that the doctrine of election is consoling to Christians because it reminds them that God's saving purposes for those who have faith in Christ cannot be thwarted by the catastrophes of history or even by their own sins, while the doctrine of free grace is a reminder to those who happen to have come to saving faith in Christ that God's saving purposes are not restricted to themselves, but are offered generously to all. The former truth rescues us from despair, the latter from complacency. The clearest statement of this paradox that I have ever heard was by my teacher at Yale, the great Lutheran theologian and ecumenist, George Lindbeck: he said, "Christian faith requires us to believe in the existence of hell, and Christian love requires us to pray that it is empty." That is, we believe that, in his justice, God has good reason to send those who refuse to accept Christ as their savior to eternal judgment; but we also believe that, in his grace, God is doing everything possible to persuade all people to accept Christ freely and thus to be fit for eternal salvation. The answer to the *theoretical* question of who will be in and who will be out is not ours to know. Our task is to keep the *practical* question before us at all times: what ought we to be doing to spread the message as widely and effectively as possible?

Hope this way of putting the issue helps.

RBS

SUBJECT: FREE WILL

Dr. Steele,

I wanted to ask you something earlier today when we were talking about God knowing everything we have done and will do in our lives before we even do any of it. A little background first: My very best friend from college last year is a pre-Christian and in the past couple weeks he has been drilling me for answers about religion, and God, and everything that goes with that, (doubt, temptation etc.). Anyhow, one of the things that comes into the conversation and that I'm not exactly sure how to answer is the question, "If God has a specific plan for all of our lives, and if He knows exactly what we're going to do far before we ever do it, then if I murder someone or steal or even lie, it was in God's will already, right?" It goes right back to what we were talking about today about being puppets or not being puppets depending on how you look at it, and not having total freedom, but having enough. How would I put into layman's terms to explain to Todd what you said today about our choices and such?

God bless!

Betty

Dear Betty,

Believe me, this is the stumper of all stumpers, and I really don't know how to explain it in a way that will make complete sense. It sounds so arbitrary and irrational just to say: "God is in complete control, and therefore although you have complete freedom and complete responsibility over your own life, you can't do anything to escape God's control." What sort of "freedom" and what sort of "responsibility" is that? Indeed, it may come as some sort of ironic comfort for you and/or your friend to know that John Wesley, the founder of Methodism and therefore the spiritual patriarch of SPU, argued in much the same way as your friend, insisting that if everything, including even our sins, is foreordained by God, then God becomes "the author of sin." And many theologians today seem more willing to say that God doesn't know (and/or cause) everything before it happens in order to protect the claim that God is loving and righteous, than to say that God knows (and causes) everything before it happens and thereby imply that he is to blame for moral and natural evil. The question then becomes, if God's knowledge of and responsibility for the future is limited by his own willingness to grant moral freedom (i.e., behavioral unpredictability) to his creatures, is God still in some *general* way sovereign? That was the purpose of the Persian rug analogy: that each of us, individually is free and able to make his or her own decisions (which decisions God has either not foreseen or at least not predestined), but that God is free and able to steer the overall course of events in a direction that brings about his grand plan for us all. Imagining how that might work is a tremendous intellectual challenge, and actually believing it is a great leap of faith. But the spiritual consequence of believing it is that one feels both morally responsible for one's actions and serenely confident in God's providential care, whereas the consequence of not believing it is that one feels either like a pawn in a cosmic game that God is playing solo or like an orphan in a godless universe. Neither of the consequences of unbelief seems to me like the right way to live a worthwhile human life, and I therefore opt for belief because its consequence is more human and humanizing.

Hope this helps.

RBS

SUBJECT: PREDESTINATION

Dr. Steele,

After sending you an email regarding predestination, I read more on the debate and realized how close my views are to those of Jacob Arminius, although I had never read much about him before. This made me question whether I had worked out my ideas on this matter on my own or whether they were influenced by the ideas of other thinkers, which had have filtered down to me through the many diverse minds of the ages. Perhaps they were a little of both. I think a lot of my ideas do come from my own thinking and reflection upon the Bible, but I feel ignorant to have made suggestions without being aware of the many people who believed and died for almost identical conclusions in ages past. Concerning the Arminians, I am still uncertain as to how different their eventual beliefs were from Arminius. I know that he considered himself a Calvinist, and I see a lot in his beliefs that resonates with me. But did his followers carry his ideas to what he would have considered extremes? You also mentioned in class that there was a logical hole in one of the points in the Remonstrance. Do you recall what it was that you mentioned? Also, do you think Arminius would have said that God specifically placed certain souls in particular times based upon a pre-knowledge of what they would do and what role they could play for Him or would he say that God simply looked to see who out of a generation would follow Him? Did this enter into the debate between the two sides? Thanks for your patience as I try to think over these questions that are so very old and much discussed yet so new and consuming for myself.

Yours in Him,

Jim

Dear Jim,

You have asked some very profound and difficult questions, and you have proposed some very fascinating solutions to matters that have puzzled believers for many centuries. It is true that many of the ideas that have occurred to you have occurred to others before you, although that does not necessarily mean that you were directly "influenced" by those authors. Indeed, some of your ideas seem almost to propose themselves to us by the very nature of the problems. At the fountainhead of Christian reflection on the questions of time/eternity and freewill/predestination is, of course, St. Augustine. And I suppose we would have to say that his meditations on these questions have shaped the thinking of everybody who has thought about them since, whether they have directly studied his writings or have simply been part of a church for which he is one of the preeminent theologians.

My own view on these, as on so many other seemingly insoluble theological conundrums, is that one must see "doctrines" not simply as "truth claims" to be defended or refuted, but as practical regulations for the right living of the life of faith. Thus, we cannot deny divine providence (and its most drastic logical consequence, divine predestination) without reducing human history itself to the level of "a tale told by an idiot, full of sound, fury, signifying nothing." That is, to assert that God is the creator of the world, that God intervened savingly at certain decisive moments in human history (e.g., the Exodus and the birth/life/death/resurrection of Jesus), and that God himself has an ultimate destination toward which his creation is moving, is to imply that ultimately all human events are somehow part of his grand strategy and are thus inherently meaningful. And that means that your life and mine are worth living (i.e., not absurd, as the above quote by Shakespeare might suggest), however full of sorrows and inexplicable disasters they may be. On the other hand, we cannot deny free will (and its most important logical consequence, namely, that we have moral responsibility for ourselves) without reducing human life to the level of a puppet show. That is, to assert that we really do make choices is to imply that, whatever God's overall strategy may be, and however inescapable his ultimate triumph may be, the actual course of events is shaped by what we do. And that, too, means that your life and mine are of genuine significance, not only to ourselves, but also to other people, and finally even to God.

Now our minds would bid us to find a nifty *theory*, which could "reconcile" the apparent logical contradiction between providence/predestination and freewill/responsibility. And lots of them have been proposed. But the point is that what looks like a contradiction "on paper" must really be resolved, not on paper, but in the living of the life of faith. For faith in the goal-directedness of history rescues us from madness and despair, and belief in the significance of human decisions rescues us from moral depravity. Spiritual wisdom consists in living confidently in the midst of history's inescapable catastrophes, and in living righteously in the face of mankind's manifold temptations. In other words, the "cash value" of the doctrines of providence and freewill is that *together* they serve to regulate the life of faith, even if they appear to cancel each other out conceptually. Which is why it is possible to live "wisely," even if we will never have life "figured out."

In answer to your question about the "logical hole" in the Arminian Remonstrance, it is that it continues to insist that salvation is possible only by divine grace at the same time that it asserts that the surrender to saving grace (i.e., faith) is a free human act. But it also wants to assert that faith itself is a divine gift. Why then do some have it and some don't—unless Calvin is right that God decrees who will have it and who won't?

RBS

SUBJECT: CAN THE SAVED LOSE THEIR SALVATION?

Dr. Steele,

I have a question that I've been brooding over for quite a while. I am very troubled by the terrible behavior and the falling away so to speak of many who profess Christ. For example, what happened to Jonathan Edwards's joy and peace at the end of his life? So many theologians end up with less Christ-likeness than they begin with. This threatens the core of my theology, my hope in Christ alone. God promises that if I seek him, I will find him. I am promised perfect peace and joy when my mind is stayed on him. What happens? Do I have any security that I will not end up rather pathetic in my walk? The Bible says I do, but what do you make of these earthly examples?

Also, how on earth could ministers presumably praying for God's wisdom and guidance end up deceived so as slave owners? It is blatantly obvious that to own slaves the American way, and treat them with cruelty is not Christ-like. Sure, society and structural evil complicates it, but God provides truth and light apart from society if we seek it, right? I have to believe Mrs. Auld should have and could have known, or I feel we have no ultimate hope.[4]

My mom said about a year ago that I could be seeking God and be misled into a cult for a time. We were discussing tongues and prophecy—which I do not know exactly what to make of, having been raised a conservative Presbyterian. How could I be misled and deceived if I was seeking God, through my Bible and prayer and the tradition of the Christian fathers? If I could be, what hope do I have?

I hope you can read between the lines to understand what I do not seem to be able to convey. Basically I am looking, I suppose, for some affirmation perhaps, of my security of sanctification.

Aubrey

Dear Aubrey,

Thank you for your very probing and difficult questions, which give voice to some of the most vexing pastoral-theological problems facing the church. Let me begin my "answer," such as it is, by noting that you have put your finger on one of the points of sharpest controversy between Calvinists and Arminian/Wesleyans. Those in the Calvinist camp solve the problem of the falling-away of those who were (apparently) saved by saying they were never really saved to begin with. This is a logical corollary of their belief that those who really are saved cannot lose their "eternal security." Those in the Arminian/Wesleyan camp solve the problem by denying that, at least in this life, people can enjoy such security, because the possibility of "backsliding" is ever-present, and the need to keep one's faith in trim is unremitting. Or, to put the same point in different terms, the Arminians regard the concept of "eternal security" as theologically dangerous, because it can tempt believers into spiritual carelessness and presumptuousness. The Arminian suspects the Calvinist of saying to himself, "If I've got it, I can't lose it, and therefore I don't need to work at keeping it." But if the Calvinist actually does lose it, then presumably he never had it to begin with. A lot hinges for the Calvinist, therefore, on *knowing* he's got it. But how can he know something that is locked in the secret counsels of God. Of course, the Calvinist finds the Arminian stance equally problematic. The Calvinist accuses the Arminian of saying to himself, "I *know* I've got it, because I have 'the assurance of faith.' Unfortunately, I have no assurance that I can keep it, and so I have to keep working at it as long as this life lasts." Which looks to the Calvinist like a very anxiety-ridden and works-dependent sort of faith.

Thus, the Calvinist concept of eternal security seems to be booby-trapped by public presumptuousness ("If I've got it, I'm sure I can't lose it") and secret anxiety ("but I don't know for sure if I've got it"). Meanwhile, astonishingly enough, the Arminian concept of the assurance of faith seems to be booby-trapped by exactly the same things: public presumptuousness ("I know I've got it") and secret anxiety ("but I have no guarantee that I can keep it"). Needless to say, this appears to be what my grandmother used to call a choice of rotten apples.

Yet the Scriptures regard saving faith as the opposite of *both* presumptuousness *and* anxiety. Thus, there must be something wrong with both formulations as they stand. And what is wrong seems to me to be that both focus their attention on the believer rather than on the Savior. Or to be more precise, both theologies try to focus the believer's attention on the Savior, but believers soon lapse back into the self-preoccupation that is characteristic of human nature, and begin to think, as the cliché goes, that "it's all about them."

It's not. It's all about God. Or rather, it's about God's work of salvation in and for us—which is to say that it's at least partly about us after all. But it's not about whether we "qualify" for salvation; rather, it's about how we "respond" to the salvation that we have been offered, despite the fact that we obviously don't qualify for it. And here is where the moral issues that you raise have their proper context. They are not tactics for insuring our spiritual well-being; they are (or ought to be) acts of gratitude for the fact that God has already insured our spiritual well-being in Christ, as well as acts of obedience to the God who, in Christ, has given us an example of what spiritual and moral wholeness is all about.

Best,

RBS

SUBJECT: GOD'S JUSTICE ECLIPSED BY HIS LOVE

Hi Dr. Steele,

When we were discussing the attributes of God a couple weeks ago, someone made the comment that it was probably easier to think of God as a God of love, rather than justice. I pondered that for a while, and I think I disagree. When I think of justice, I think of logical, laid-out rules that have consequences (maybe the reward-and-punishment kind of thing we were discussing). This seems much easier to think of: Do this, and you get into heaven. Don't do it, and you go to hell.

But the notion of a God who is all-pursuing, all-consuming love—that's scary. To imagine the kind of love that would give up His Son for all, that wants to be in relationship with me, and loves me because of, not in spite of, my brokenness, is hard to believe sometimes. Worth every minute of believing it, no doubt, but difficult at times, to say the least. I doubt the comment was meant to go so far, but my brain kind of took it and ran with it. Not that I'm suggesting that one should forget about the justice thing, but it somehow must be eclipsed by Love, at least in my mind.

And it seems the whole predestination argument comes back to love and people's perception/ideas of what God's love looks like: Is it love that grants us freedom? Or a love that knows better than we do what will happen, and has everything planned out already? A little of both, I suspect. I appreciate the comment made by Lena that God doesn't make it clear for a reason. It—well, all our class sessions, really—have reminded me of some lines by one of my favorite authors, Rainer Maria Rilke: "Try to love the questions themselves. Do not now look for answers. They cannot now be given to you because you could not live them. It is a question of experiencing everything. At present you need to live the question. Perhaps you will gradually, without even noticing it, find yourself experiencing the answer, some distant day."

I am loving the questions at the moment. It's good to ponder and be free to not have answers. So there are some of my random thoughts that this class has generated.

Have a blessed day!

Jeri

Dear Jeri,

This is surely one of the most profound and beautifully crafted emails I have ever received from a student, and in one sense I don't have much to say in response to your reflections besides "Amen!" But even though I may not have much to add to what you have said so clearly, you certainly deserve the favor of an acknowledgment.

First, I think you are exactly right to say that "the notion of a God who is all-pursuing, all-consuming love" is scary, and much scarier than the notion of a God who operates according to some clearly delineated set of rules and regulations. The reason is that rules generally tell you what you should *not* do. And as long as you are not doing what the rules have forbidden, you can assume you're safe. But love forces you to figure out for yourself on a case-by-case basis what you *should* do. It is therefore much more demanding and open-ended than justice. It is not a question of avoiding a limited set number of sins, but of undertaking an unlimited set of responsibilities. With love, you're never "off the hook"—though in another sense you don't want to be "off the hook," because that would be equivalent to no longer being "in relation."

Second, you are again exactly right in wanting to see the doctrine of predestination as a way of expressing thanks for God's unconquerable, redemptive love, rather than as a way of "explaining" everything that occurs in the world. The former is a religious concept, while the latter is a cold (and, to my way of thinking, very implausible) metaphysical one. For the purpose of organizing one's life on the basis of the grace that God has given us in Jesus Christ, we don't need any "explanations" of why things are as they are. What we need is a motivation for living faithful lives in the midst of the tragedies and confusions that face us daily. Predestination is theological code language for the belief that nothing can occur that God cannot use for God's loving, redemptive purposes. That is a far different thing from asserting that God "causes" (or even "permits") everything that happens.

Third, I too love Rilke, and especially that very famous line from *Letters to a Young Poet* about "loving the questions." And I'm extremely gratified that you believe that most of our class sessions arouse in your mind questions that are worth pondering lovingly, rather than answering too quickly and formulaically.

Warm regards,

RBS

SUBJECT: IS THERE AN UPPER LIMIT TO "PERFECTION"?[5]

Dr. Steele,

While turning over today's discussion in my mind, I had a thought (and just one). As we were talking about Edwards's view of eternity as a continual process of coming closer to God, I kept thinking that I had heard this before. In a way, I guess I had because it has echoes of Dante and Augustine (among others), but I realized I was thinking of a talk Dr. Maddox gave at First Free about entire sanctification. I am probably butchering the wonderful explanation of entire sanctification that Dr. Maddox gave, but it seemed to be an earthly state in which the believer has, according to the level of her maturity, aligned her will to that of God. Naturally, this alignment is limited by the believer's knowledge of God, but as that knowledge increases so does the believer's ability (and, even, in a way that does make her prior desire deficient, her desire) to align her will with God's. (I would like to state that I am not attempting to explain entire sanctification to you. I am sure you have an infinitely better handle on it than I. But thought I probably should explain my own misunderstanding of it so you could see from whence the following illogic stems.)

Thus, by blithely combining my theologians (Wesley and Edwards both deserve better), it would seem that heaven is really a continuation (minus the presence of sin, adding the full presence of God) of something that really starts here on earth. This seems to fit into (and now I am combining not only my theologians but my classes in a fairly irresponsible way) what Dr. Lemcio taught about the way eternal life is described in the Gospel of John. Eternal life is not something we gain after we die, but something that begins when we come to know Christ and align our wills with his. Eternity is not something distant (in at least one sense), but a process in which we are currently engaged. This seems to give what I am doing now, at this moment, a different perspective.

Sally

Dear Sally,

I think your synthesis of Wesley/Edwards/St. John is a first-rate piece of theologizing, or to be more precise, of "eschatologizing." You have put several profound Christian convictions, as formulated from several of the greatest minds and hearts in the tradition, to work in a highly imaginative and provocative way. We know, for one thing, that we are called to "perfection," but we also know that even the most "perfect" life cannot stand still. We know, further, that "eternal life" is what we have when we know the God revealed in Jesus Christ, and that such life is as deathless as Christ himself. Which is to say, it begins in us here and now, when we first acquire "saving knowledge" of him, and it cannot be terminated when we die, precisely because it is *his* life in us and our life in *him*. We know, further still, that to acquire this "eternal life" (a.k.a. "participation in the divine nature") we must, as you say, "align our will" with God's will. But we also know that at a deeper level we are able to do so only because God enables and empowers us to do so. And we know, finally, that when God begins a good work in a soul, God brings that work to completion—even if the work of endowing a soul with eternal life takes an eternity! The consequence of this chain of reasoning is a picture of heaven in which the soul's approach to God is "asymptotic," always getting nearer, always enjoying the process of getting nearer, and never experiencing frustration over the fact that one never quite "arrives," because each step in the process is, at one and the same time, the exquisite ("perfect") culmination of all the preceding steps and the necessary precondition for all of the following ones. To revert to my trite analogy, each heavenly "glass of lemonade" quenches the thirst for God you had a moment ago and yet awakens a new thirst—which will itself be quenched by the next glass. The "lemonade" never runs out, and the only requirement for getting your next glass of it is that you receive it thankfully from one of your fellow angels, and then turn around and pour a glass for somebody else.

Cheers,

RBS

NOTES

1 Cf. Alan P. F. Sell, *The Great Debate: Calvinism, Arminianism and Salvation* (Grand Rapids: Baker Book House, 1983).

2 See, e.g., Carl Bangs, *Arminius: A Study in the Dutch Reformation* (Eugene, OR: Wipf and Stock Publishers, 1998); Joseph G. Haroutunian, *Piety Versus Moralism: The Passing of the New England Theology* (New York: Henry Holt and Co., 1932); Nathan O. Hatch in *The Democratization of American Christianity* (New Haven and London: Yale University Press, 1989); Thomas A. Langford, *Practical Divinity: Theology in the Wesleyan Tradition* (Nashville: Abingdon Press, 1983); Randy L. Maddox, *Responsible Grace: John Wesley's Practical Theology* (Nashville: Kingswood Books/Abingdon Press, 1994); John T. McNeill, *The History and Character of Calvinism* (London, Oxford, and New York: Oxford University Press, 1954); Thomas C. Oden, ed., *Phoebe Palmer: Selected Writings*, Sources of American Spirituality (New York and Mahwah: Paulist Press, 1988). Thomas A.

Langford, *Practical Divinity: Theology in the Wesleyan Tradition* (Nashville: Abingdon Press, 1983).

3 Daniel L. Migliore, *Faith Seeking Understanding: An Introduction to Christian Theology* (Grand Rapids: William B. Eerdmans, 1991), ch. 4.

4 Mrs. Auld is a character in Frederick Douglass, *Narrative of the Life of Frederick Douglass* (New York: Dover Publications, 1995), who illustrates Douglass's contention that slavery has a morally corrosive effect, not only on slaves, but also on slave-owners. She had owned no slaves until Douglass came into her possession, and Douglass tells us that when he first arrived in her home he was "astonished at her goodness." But, he asserts, her goodness was nothing more than innocence, and "the fatal poison of irresponsible power . . . soon commenced its infernal work. That cheerful eye, under the influence of slavery, soon became red with rage; that voice, made all of sweet accord, changed to one of harsh and horrid discord; and that angelic face gave place to that of a demon" (19).

5 The following email illustrates how a particularly gifted student will synthesize material from different courses and sources. She was at the time taking my course, "Christianity in America," in which we study the thought of Jonathan Edwards. She was also taking a course on the Gospel of John with Dr. Eugene Lemcio, and had recently heard a chapel talk at "First Free" (the campus church) by Dr. Randy Maddox on Wesley's eschatology. Here she explores the connections between these disparate ideas.

CHAPTER 5

FAITH
AND
FOSSILS

In this chapter, we wrestle with the question of whether Christianity and modern science are compatible. My answer is that they are *not in*-compatible. To accept the truth of one does not force you to deny the truth of the other—*provided you don't use the rules by which either ascertains the kind of truth appropriate to it in order to test the validity of the other's claims.* Christianity and science occupy different logical terrain. They represent different ways of looking at the world. They answer different kinds of questions. They analyze different kinds of evidence, and each has its own way of analyzing what it considers to be evidence relevant to itself. Moreover, they play different roles in human life. If you respect these differences, you don't have to settle the alleged "conflict" between them; the conflict simply disappears.

Students sometimes ask me, "Did Noah have dinosaurs on his ark?" They want to believe that the Bible is "true," but they also want to know how its truth can be squared with the fossil record. And knowing me to be a professor of Christian theology, they expect me not only to say yes, but also to explain how Noah solved the logistical problems such cargo would have posed. What's more, they figure I can explain how one hundred million year-old fossils can lie buried in a six thousand year-old earth. So I am faced with a dilemma: I can either scandalize their faith by denying the literal "truth" of the Bible, or insult their intelligence by trotting out the "theories" of the creationists. There is a third alternative. When a question can have no clear *answer* it may be because it has no clear *meaning*. What is that third alternative?

For starters, let's look at three important features of our ordinary language. First, for a statement to be true or false—for it to be a "truth claim" or "proposition"—it must have a determinate meaning. Second, for a statement to have meaning, it must have a home in a broader swath of human discourse—what the philosopher Ludwig Wittgenstein called a "language game."[1] But third, for a statement to be meaningful, it need not be a truth claim; that is, it need not be either truth or false. Many religious statements are like that.

Consider an example. In church we pray, "Lord, have mercy!" This is a deeply meaningful prayer for us Christians, expressing our sorrow for sin and our trust in divine mercy. But, grammatically, it is a petition, not a proposition. It *assumes* something (that we are sinners), and it *asks* for something (that

God might forgive us), but it doesn't really *assert* anything. So the prayer, "Lord, have mercy" has meaning for a Christian, but it is neither true nor false.

Let's take this a step further. As we've seen, when Christians pray, "Lord, have mercy," they assume that certain things are true. These truths can be stated as propositions: "We are sinners. God is merciful." Yet for such propositions to be meaningful, they must be embedded in a much larger context of speech and life—the narratives of Christian Scripture, the rituals of Christian worship, the practices of Christian discipleship and fellowship. To utter the statement, "I am a sinner," *apart* from that context is not to utter a religious truth; but neither is it to utter a falsehood. It is simply to talk nonsense. The statement simply "misfires."[2]

Consider the following thought experiment: A minister suddenly interrupts the celebration of the Lord's Supper to discuss, with perfect seriousness, the championship baseball game that the home team won the night before. The congregation is understandably puzzled—even if the minister gets all the "facts" right. He is making true statements, and about a topic whose significance the congregation would readily grant in another context (say, coffee hour). But in *that* context, what he is saying is simply jarring to them—all the more so if he seems *unaware* that what he is saying is jarring to them. The mere fact that his sports coverage is "accurate" doesn't make it relevant or meaningful. He has violated the logic of Christian worship by introducing extraneous material. He is mixing his language games—and accordingly, seems a bit crazy.[3]

Now we're ready to address the question of whether there were dinosaurs on Noah's ark. However piously intended, it is logically absurd, another case of the unwarranted commingling of two language games, this time paleontology and biblical narrative. Therefore one can't answer the question with a yes or no, because it assumes that what counts as a "fact" in one context must automatically count as a "fact" in the other. This is simply wrong. The context in which the story of Noah appears is the grand biblical testimony to God's abiding care for creation. And the theological truth of the Noah story depends on the overall plausibility of the biblical testimony—something that must be established on grounds other than its alleged "accuracy" as natural science. Theological convictions have no logical home in scientific discourse; neither can scientific truth claims be imported without further ado into religious discourse. There is simply no direct traffic between these two logical domains.

We should read the Bible for what it *is*—a richly textured library of ancient writings and, at the same time, but much more importantly, the Word of God to the people of God—and not for what it *isn't*—a pile of undifferentiated factoids demanding our assent. We have to pay close attention to the literary context and theological purpose of every biblical passage if we are to delight in and profit from scripture's artistic richness and spiritual depth. We need to realize that trying to prove that biblical testimonies must be "historically accurate" in order to be theologically true is not an act of intellectually responsible faith, but a sign of fetishistic attachment to the "killing letter" (cf. 2 Corinthians 3:6), a case of uncritical devotion to a positivistic view of "truth" that modern science itself now rejects. We must learn how to spot red herrings and category mistakes—questions which are not only unanswerable on empirical grounds, but logically meaningless and foreign to the kind of knowledge the Bible offers and the kind of faith it promotes.

This isn't to deny that the Bible contains a great deal of accurate and interesting information about the past. It does. It's only to say that the Bible isn't interested in historical information for its own sake, that it isn't driven by scientific curiosity or antiquarian nostalgia. Its aim is to communicate theological convictions, the validity of which is borne out in the day-to-day business of faithful Christian discipleship. All the "information" about ancient people, places, and events the Bible happens to contain is there, not to prove to later generations what fine biographers, geographers, and historians its authors were, and thus to "verify" its religious claims. It's there because the biblical authors believed in a God who reveals himself in certain real people (sometimes very holy ones, and sometimes quite unholy), in certain determinate places (sometimes very exalted ones, and sometimes quite humble), and in certain actual events (sometimes very dramatic ones, and sometimes quite ordinary). To bear witness to the presence of God in this world, the biblical writers employ a wide variety of literary forms: sagas, parables, proverbs, songs, prayers, letters, prophecies, visions, and so forth. Each of these forms has its own inner logic, its own stylistic conventions, its own terms of art, and its own way of attesting to what the people of faith, then as now, experience and observe about the world around them and the world within them. This is what makes Bible study such a grand adventure: it requires us to learn how each of these literary forms does its specific kind of theological work. To think that the religious credibility of this variegated literature is dependent on the capacity of latter-day historians and archaeologists to prove that the biblical text doesn't contain any "mistakes" or "inconsistencies"—as if it were a sort of camcording of ancient events[4]—is misguided. It springs from a failure to appreciate the logical structure and rhetorical form of the various kinds of religious discourse contained in the Bible's pages. We must learn to read the Bible *theologically*, that is, as a chorus of human voices singing various parts in a grand opera of divine love.

SUBJECT: NOAH AND DINOSAURS

Dr. Steele:

I actually have two questions for you. My first one concerns Genesis. I was just wondering why God spared Noah in the wipeout of mankind and all other creatures of the earth. Despite Noah's righteousness and covenant with God, didn't God realize that if some people were left alive (Noah and his family), they would eventually disobey him and wreck the world with sin all over again? My other question is one that my father and I were very curious about. Did dinosaurs *really* exist in history, or is it a mythical thing because man couldn't possibly coexist with dinosaurs if God created man first?

Melanie

Dear Melanie,

Thanks for sending these questions. As for the first, if we affirm that God is all-knowing, then presumably we can't deny that God knew what the consequences of saving Noah would be, namely, that sin would soon re-enter his world. As a matter of fact, it did so almost as soon as Noah and his family got off the ark, as the rather puzzling but certainly scandalous story of Noah's bout of drunkenness (Genesis 9:20–28) suggests. As one preacher noted, here Noah had the whole world before him, newly washed clean of sin by the flood, and he enjoyed almost limitless possibilities since he had the place all to himself and his family. But what did he do? Planted vines, made wine, took off his clothes, drank to the point of passing out, and then was discovered naked by his sons. A discouraging picture of humanity, to say the least. But the point of the story of the ark is precisely that God *does* know that people will go on sinning, but has pledged never again to resort to universal destruction as a means of correcting the problem. See his promise in Genesis 8:21a: "I will never again curse the ground because of humankind, for the inclination of the human heart is evil from youth; nor will I ever again destroy every living creature as I have done."

Second, the existence of fossils, including most dramatically those of the dinosaurs (and of many other creatures, some of which seem to be hundreds of millions of years older than those of the dinosaurs) is one of the reasons that most modern scientists feel that the Bible's chronology cannot be taken literally. One seventeenth century churchman calculated from the Bible that the world was created in the year 4004 BC. But twentieth century geologists would put the date of the earth's formation at something like 4 to 5 billion years ago—rather older! On this view, dinosaurs are said to have appeared maybe 245 million years ago, and to have gone extinct about 65 million years ago. They were long gone by the time humans appeared, about 2 or 3 million years ago. Now, what are we to make of this apparent discrepancy?

I, for one, do not regard dinosaurs as "mythical things," although I am not a scientist and am not qualified to rule on the accuracy of the current scientific theories of the earth's age or of the dates at which various creatures evolved or went extinct. In a sense, I accept those theories "on faith." That is, I trust the reliability of the methods that scientists use to support them. True, I have no professional competence in that area, but I see no reason to believe that the scientific community has concocted the whole thing as a gigantic fraud on the public. As for what my acceptance of the scientific data does to my faith in the reliability of the Bible, I can tell you in two words: absolutely nothing. For I do not read the bible for the purpose of gaining information about the age of the earth or the evolution and extinction of animals and plants, but for the purpose of knowing how God deals with humanity. And the latter sort of knowledge is not affected at all by what the scientists tell us about the age of the world.

Cheers,

RBS

SUBJECT: CONCERNING ADAM AND EVE

Dear Dr. Steele,

My wife and I were visiting our home church this weekend. The pastor was speaking on the purpose of salvation. He went on to explain the thing called sin, and referred to passages found in Romans chapter 5. In

Romans 5:15 it states: "For if the many died through the one man's trespass, much more surely have the grace of God and the free gift in the grace of the one man, Jesus Christ, abounded for many." Again in Romans 5:18–19 it states: "Therefore just as one man's trespass led to condemnation for all, so one man's act of righteousness leads to justification and life for all. For just as by the one man's disobedience the many were made sinners, so by the one man's obedience the many will be made righteous." I understand that this is far from an excuse for sinning, and that we make that choice, but my question is: Did not the origin of sin begin in Adam, and for that matter, is not the account of Adam and Eve a historical one? It seems to me, that the way Paul is speaking, he would not think of the account as "imaginative."[5]

In His Steps,

Jack

Dear Jack,

Thanks for you post. Yes, Paul probably did assume that the Adam and Eve story was "historical." That is, he probably believed it was an account of "real" people in "real" time. Most Christians have assumed this, and many still do. Nor am I personally interested in denying it. The problem is that there are many people in the world today—some influenced by modern science, some by modern skepticism and atheism (which are not by any means the same thing as modern science!)—who think they have good reason for denying the religious truth of the Bible as a whole because they have reasons for calling into question the historicity of the creation account, just as they have reasons for calling into question the facticity of the Bible's cosmology. (The Bible also says that God created a "firmament" above the earth, that is, a solid dome which created a flat, open space within the watery primeval chaos, a space that we call "the world." The sun, moon, and stars are said to be inserted in this dome. See Genesis 1:6–8. Does anybody today take *that* cosmological picture literally—a picture of a flat earth with a solid revolving dome overhead? Almost nobody does. But does the religious truth of the biblical creation account depend on the "accuracy" of that picture? Not at all.) What I am saying is simply that the religious truth of the Bible can, to a certain extent, be detached from the ancient worldview by means of which it was originally presented, such that, if the ancient worldview proves "inaccurate," that does not logically entail the refutation of the Bible's religious truth. And the "religious truth" of the Adam and Eve story is the claim that all human beings are sinners destined to die. This claim is key to Paul's argument in Romans, which holds out the possibility that, through faith in the Second Adam (i.e., Jesus Christ) people can be redeemed from their sin and its tragic consequence, and ushered into a new community whose members are marked by righteousness and promised a share in Christ's resurrection. Does accepting the promise of righteousness and eternal life in Christ depend on our being able to recognize that we are sinners destined to die, and incapable of saving ourselves from sin and death by our good works? Yes, indeed it does. And that is precisely what being "in Adam" means, theologically. But does the promise of righteousness and eternal life in Christ depend on our being able to "prove" that Adam and Eve were historical figures? No, thank God it does not, because then if someone were able to "disprove" that Adam and Eve were historical figures, our faith would be in vain. My point, then, is not to attack the historicity of the Adam and Eve story as such, but simply to show that certain religious convictions central to the Christian faith (i.e., humanity's fallenness and mortality, and the promise of righteousness and eternal life in Christ) do not hinge on the historicity of the Adam and Eve story. That is, those convictions remain plausible even if you take Genesis 1–3 to be an "imaginative" depiction of our situation, rather than a "scientific" or "historical" account. [Note: For Migliore, "imaginative" does not mean "imaginary"! He does not treat the story of Adam and Eve as if it were no more than a fable about unicorns or an alcoholic nightmare about pink elephants.]

RBS

* * * * *

Dr. Steele,

I was reading your email on Adam and Eve,[6] and how we need not regard that story as "historical." I agree with this. However, if we don't have faith that the events actually happened, then what would be the basis of our faith? If the events in the Bible didn't happen, then what becomes of other beliefs central to Christianity? I hope this is not too trivial a question.

Matthew

Dear Matthew:

This is an excellent question, not trivial at all! But please do not assume that because I am willing to concede that *some* stories in the Bible *may* be "imaginative portrayals" of the human condition rather than historical records, I must be asserting that *all* of them *must* be. Not at all! I entirely agree that there has to be some core of historical "fact" to the Bible, and that even if that core does not include the Garden of Eden story, surely it has to include the essential narratives of the Old Testament, such as the liberation of the Hebrews from bondage in Egypt, the giving of the Law, and occupation of the Promised Land, as well as the equally essential narratives in the New Testament of the life, teachings, death, and resurrection of Jesus of Nazareth and the founding and expansion of the Christian Church. As St. Paul puts it, "If Christ has not been raised, then our proclamation is in vain and your faith has been in vain" (1 Corinthians 15:14). Hence, the question is, what stories in the Bible are meant as records of "real" historical events and what ones are meant as "imaginative portrayals" of the human condition in general? I'm not sure that we can make an absolute, once-and-for-all differentiation here, but I do think we can often tell one from the other by certain literary cues in the biblical writings themselves.

Best,

RBS

SUBJECT: DOES THE THEORY OF EVOLUTION CONTRADICT THE BIBLE?

Dr. Steele,

Hi! My name is Carla, and I am writing a paper on creationism for an English class I have here at SPU. I was wondering if you would be willing to offer any insights you have into a couple issues. I am mainly struggling with the "age of the earth" controversy and how evolutionary theory and the Bible may or may not work together. Any tidbits you would be willing to share would help me expand my understanding of the subject. Thank you in advance for your help!

Have a great day!

Carla

Dear Carla:

In my opinion, the alleged "contradiction" between the biblical account of creation and contemporary biological and geological theories about the age of the earth and the evolution of species is more apparent than real. That is, when the Bible speaks of "creation," it is making a theological affirmation about the nature and purposes of God and the relationship between God and the universe, about who made the world and why. That is why, in Scripture, references to creation almost always occur in the context of acts of praise. Theologically, nothing much hinges on how the universe works or how long it has been in existence. But these latter are precisely the kinds of questions that scientists are interested in. And they are perfectly good questions. But the mere fact that the answers scientists give to those questions appear, at one level, not to square with the testimony of the Bible is, I believe, of no religious significance at all, since the biblical testimony was not really meant to give answers to those questions. That is, the authors of the Bible used the best "science" at their disposal—ancient Egyptian, Mesopotamian, and Greek science—as the "outward dress," so to speak, in which to present their witness to divine creativity and providence. It was the best—indeed, the only— "science" available, and they made use of it. Yet the truth of their religious witness in no way hinges on the adequacy of ancient science—but neither is it contradicted by the findings of modern science.

There is, however, one point at which contemporary believers have some cause for alarm when faced with modern scientific theories of origins, namely in the assumption which sometimes accompanies those theories that there is no overarching divine purpose, no ultimate moral government operating in, with, under, through, around, above, and in spite of natural phenomena and human history. Scientists, of course, can't prove that there is not, any more than believers can prove that there is. That is a matter of faith. But when scientists move from descriptions of natural and historical processes (which is their proper business) to metaphysical explanations which deny divine providence simply because providence can't be proven, then they have said something which is contradictory to the Christian faith. The key point, however, is that such a denial, even when made by scientists, is no longer within the strict domain of empirical science.

Best,

RBS

NOTES

1 Ludwig Wittgenstein, *Philosophical Investigations*, 3rd ed., trans. G. E. M. Anscombe (New York: Macmillan Co., 1958), *passim*.

2 Cf. J. L. Austin, *How to Do Things with Words*, 2nd ed. Edited by J. O. Urmson and Marina Sbisà (Cambridge: Harvard University Press, 1975), 16–18.

3 Cf. the following anecdote from Plutarch's life of the Roman statesman, Cato the Elder: "Whenever his opinion was called for on any subject, he invariably concluded with the words, 'And furthermore it is my opinion that Carthage must be destroyed!'" *Makers of Rome: Nine Lives by Plutarch*, trans. Ian Scott-Kilvert (Harmondsworth: Penguin Books, 1968), 150. This comes close to being the exception that proves the rule (although Cato's famous remark is not, grammatically, a proposition). For Cato's point in repeatedly stating that opinion during Senate debates on "other" matters was precisely that the political danger presented by Carthage *was* the wider context in which every other matter had to be set. The rhetorical power of his constant refrain was due to the fact that he was aware of the relevance of an issue that his colleagues preferred to ignore—but knew they couldn't.

4 I owe this vivid analogy to my colleague, Frank Spina.

5 Jack is here referring to an extensive classroom conversation on Daniel L. Migliore's statement, "The biblical stories of the Garden of Eden and the 'fall' are imaginative portrayals of the goodness of creation and the universality of sin rather than historical accounts of sin's origin." *Faith Seeking*

Understanding (Grand Rapids: Wm B. Eerdmans Publishing Co., 1991), 134.

6 This post was a follow-up to the previous exchange, which had been sent to the entire class in which both Jack and Matthew were enrolled.

CHAPTER 6

KEEPING THE FAITH IN A POSTMODERN WORLD

The old joke goes that there are only two kinds of people in the world: those who believe there are only two kinds of people in the world, and those who don't. Many believe that, with respect to religion, there are only two kinds of people. One kind regards religious beliefs as absolute truth claims, which must be held passionately to be held properly, and which should be commended fervently to others. The other kind regards religious beliefs as expressions of the upbringing and interests of those who hold them, and deems any attempt by believers to proselytize as presumptuous and invasive. We'll call the first group "absolutists" and the second group "relativists." I'm convinced there's a third option, which mediates between the other two. Those who take this view, whom I'll call "soft perspectivists,"[1] regard religious beliefs as warranted convictions, which deserve and command the believer's passionate commitment, and which may properly be defended and recommended to others. Yet these convictions must never be imposed coercively on others, and the manner in which they are formulated must always be left open for revision—open to new moral and spiritual insights and responsive to new historical developments. Let's look at each of these positions a bit more closely.

1. Absolutism. The religious absolutist or "true believer"[2] is one who affirms a particular set of religious beliefs—and affirms them *passionately*. Indeed, the passion with which he affirms his beliefs is as important to him as the objective truth of the particular beliefs he affirms. This is because the passion gives him great moral and spiritual power—power to resist temptation, to withstand opposition, to make great sacrifices, and to face the uncertainties of life. Conversely, he believes that if you deny that religious convictions are objectively true (i.e., true for everyone, including those who reject them), you drain religion of its power. Note that what marks the absolutist is not the specific religious beliefs he holds, but his view on the role that the holding of religious beliefs plays in life. So you could be a Christian . . . or a Muslim . . . or a Jewish absolutist. If you were a Christian absolutist, you could be a Calvinist . . . or a Catholic . . . or a Methodist absolutist. Different kinds of absolutists believe different things. And if there are three different kinds of absolutists in a room, the sparks will fly! But the sparks will fly not just because they disagree about their beliefs, but also because they share the assumption that somebody must be right (and naturally each thinks it is himself) and that everybody else must be wrong. On doctrinal grounds, they may hate each other; but each respects the passion with which the others hold their views. Conversely, each may despise those members of his own religious community who seem willing to avoid questions of religious *truth* for the sake of public *peace*: for by making concessions on the truth of religion, they neutralize its power. In the absolutist's scale of values, lukewarm orthodoxy is just as reprehensible as heresy or infidelity—maybe more so.

2. Relativism. For the religious relativist, religious absolutism has two fatal weaknesses. It asserts truth claims it can't prove, and it often tries to coerce people it can't convince. The relativist sees that absolutists disagree—and disagree passionately—amongst themselves. But he is struck by the fact that there is no one to adjudicate the debate impartially, no set of universally accepted moral or metaphysical principles by which the specific beliefs and practices of each party could be assessed to the satisfaction of all. That's why debates among absolutists over beliefs so often degenerate into violence. What's more, the relativist believes that the "truths" which absolutists hold often simply reflect their background or their social, cultural, and political interests. They aren't so much truth claims as rationalizations of the selfish aims of those who hold them—instruments of self-assertion and self-justification. And because truth itself is a will-o'-the wisp, the exercise of coercive power by one group of true believers on others is deeply immoral. In despair of ever knowing the truth, the relativist settles for seeking peace among the squabbling absolutists. He tries to get them to renounce, not their beliefs, but their passionate commitment to their beliefs. He can't see that they are as committed to their passionate commitment as they arc to the beliefs to which they are passionately committed! Nor, perhaps, can he see that he himself is passionately committed to the belief that passionate commitment to beliefs is dangerous. He may be certain that it's morally preferable to make peace with uncertainty than to profess as certain something you can't prove. But can *he* prove *that*?

3. Soft Perspectivism. What marks perspectivism is that it refuses to choose between "truth" and "peace," as if either were worth having without the other, as if human flourishing were possible without both. Perspectivism acknowledges, and even celebrates, the fact that the postmodern world is religiously pluralistic. Yet it denies that pluralism entails relativism, that the sociological fact that people have different beliefs prevents them from communicating or respectfully witnessing to one another. It denies, too, that the outcome of such dialogue must be a syncretistic blur—a hodgepodge of spiritual platitudes and general moral "values," which everybody can assent to but which nobody will be changed by. It understands the metaphysical density and moral gravity of each religion's non-negotiable truth claims, and although it leaves open the possibility that these claims may need to be reformulated as time goes by, in response to new circumstances and insights, it doesn't conclude despairingly that there is no ultimate truth to be known or that religious teachings are just ideological props for naked self-interest.

But can a convinced perspectivist really be a committed Christian? Doesn't the perspectivist's willingness to subject her supposedly non-negotiable convictions to testing and reformulation in light of other religious views and in response to changing historical realities represent a quiet apostasy? Isn't it just a mildly pious form of relativism—one that refuses to face facts? I don't think so—and here's why:

The Christian gospel contains within itself the demand that those who profess it shall refuse to identify it with their own preferred way of formulating it. That is, Christianity claims to be based on divine self-revelation, not human aspiration or religious experience. It doesn't deny the value of human aspiration and religious experience. Indeed, it asserts that divine self-revelation *prompts* a certain kind of human aspiration and *evokes* a characteristic array of religious experiences. But it asserts that God always stands in judgment of those to whom he reveals himself, and insists that they take account of how their own sinfulness skews the way they pray, preach, worship, and live. The Christian gospel itself rejects the tendency of absolutists to equate the act of believing with the object of belief, and requires believers to cultivate an attitude of fearless self-criticism and ceaseless repentance. Yet it also rejects the tendency of relativists to suspend belief for fear of believing wrongly, and promises believers that their commitment will be rewarded by Christ's abiding presence and continuing self-disclosure. The early church attested to this in the very form of its New Testament canon: holding "one faith," it nevertheless canonized four gospels; following "one Lord," it nevertheless heeded many apostolic witnesses (cf. Ephesians 4:4–6). My hope is that you will hear the simple melody of the gospel, as it is sung by a diverse chorus of voices.

SUBJECT: POSTMODERNISM IN THE CHURCH

Dr. Steele,

I have been reading in a book called *The Disconnected Generation: Saving Our Youth from Self-Destruction* by Josh McDowell (Word Publishing Group, 2000), and I had a question for you. Because most teenagers have a postmodern way of thinking, just because they don't know anything else (and the way that the book defines postmodernism is a worldview characterized by the belief that truth is created rather than discovered) do you think that the gap created by postmodernism between the church and the people is going to get worse? Do you think that the church is trying to deal with that kind of thinking? Do you think that this different way of thinking between the church and the people who have a postmodern mindset is going to create problems for the church? Or should I just stop worrying about this and let God take care of it? You know, I guess it is fun for me to think on these things, and then I feel like God gives me a gentle reminder that He transcends all of this nonsense. What is postmodernism compared to God?

Charles

Dear Charles,

These are important questions, and I wish I had as good an answer for them as they deserve. Unfortunately, I do not. However, let me make a few statements, aphoristic and perhaps even enigmatic in nature, to push you to think further about your questions. These statements are not, however, meant to foreclose further conversation between us on these matters. Rather, they are meant to prod your reflections and to stimulate an on-going conversation between us—a conversation from which, I suspect, I will learn more from you than you will from me.

1. It is said that truth is created rather than discovered, and that it is "created" by people for the purpose of furthering their own interests and legitimizing their own preferences.[3] But if it is true that truth is created, then the statement that truth is created must itself be a "created" truth, that is, a byproduct of some self-serving ideology.

2. Who stands to benefit most from the idea that truth is created? Those who have a deep interest in detaching people from their long-standing commitments and in stimulating them to try out as many options in life as possible. And who are they? Those who want to sell us things. In short, there is a more than accidental connection between postmodernism and consumerism.

3. If, however, the statement, "All truth is created," is something that the postmodernists have observed in the world as it is, i.e., a truth that they have "discovered" rather than one they themselves have "created," then they have contradicted their own claim that all truth is created. And thus postmodernism dies the death of all forms of skepticism and unchecked relativism, namely the death of self-refutation.

4. But the *practical* question of how we minister to people who continue to think in postmodern/consumerist terms remains. There are two quick observations I would make on that. First, in its claim that each self has its own story,

postmodernism leaves a curious opening to those of us who believe our personal story has meaning precisely *because* it is linked with the "old, old story of Jesus and his love." That story is apt to get a better hearing today than a generation ago, when everybody was madly searching for some irrefutable "foundation" for all truth, a foundation not resting upon the peculiarities and particularities of anybody's perspective. Put differently, Christians have a better chance today of showing that although they do, indeed, have but one of many perspectives (as opposed to an irrefutable "Absolute Truth" that reasonable people would "have" to believe if they only understood it), there are certain things (about God and about themselves) that people can *only* see if they are looking from *this* perspective. Second, the value of seeing such things will not be apparent to people who don't yet see them (in Christian terms, "the unconverted") unless the lives of the "converted" *show* it. The Christian virtues, about which we have been talking in class, are ways of *displaying* the truth of the Gospel to the world, and although the failure of Christians to manifest the virtues does not of itself falsify the Gospel, it can nullify its salvific effect for those who see us as hypocrites.

Let's keep talking about these highly important matters.

RBS

SUBJECT: DROWNING IN RELATIVISM

Dr. Steele,

I wanted to bounce a couple thoughts off of you. It seems that many beliefs today are a backlash (or corrective, I suppose) of modernity. With all the reliance on reason, measurement, knowledge, ethical analysis, etc. that people had to reach a point where they found that truth cannot always be found by means of mere reason. We now see relativism drowning our culture. If reason cannot ultimately determine the same truth for everyone, then perhaps truth is different for each person. What do you think?

Regarding the quote, "the destination is the journey," it seems that this is true to a degree for Christians. Whereas many believers would like to say, "Once you're saved, you're 'there,'" so that heaven is the endpoint of the journey, the truth is that the life of the believer does continue as a journey. It is kind of like what you said about Christian perfection: "If you think that you have reached Christian perfection, then you have proved that you have not." Thoughts?

In Christ,

Sunny

Dear Sunny,

Thanks for this thoughtful and provocative post. As to contemporary relativism—it manifests itself most obviously in morals and theology, but there are even signs of it in the natural and social sciences—I think you are exactly on target when you say that it is a reaction against Enlightenment rationalism. Or to be more precise, against Enlightenment "foundationalism," i.e., the idea that there is some Absolute Truth, valid for everyone, which the human mind is presumed to be capable of apprehending, if the proper method is employed. During the eighteenth century, the preferred methods according to which this search for Absolute Truth was to be conducted were those of mathematics and the newly emerging natural sciences. During the nineteenth and early twentieth centuries, an anti-rationalist reaction set in, and different methods were proposed, such as the social sciences, psychological introspection and mystical experience. But even this "reaction" still presumed that Absolute Truth was there to be known. Eventually, just about every conceivable method was tried, but no Absolute Truth (i.e., a set of moral norms and/or scientific principles to which all people of "reason and good will" could assent) was found. This has led in recent years to the so-called "post-modern" reaction—a reaction against Enlightenment rationalism and Romantic irrationalism alike. This reaction often leads people into sheer relativism, i.e., the belief that "knowledge" is little more than ideological justification of human interests. Hence knowledge is "different for each person," because each person (and group) has his or her (or their) own interests. Unfortunately, at that point it becomes very hard to know what to say about God, because the Christian presumption is that God is Absolute Truth.

Finally, yes, I poked a bit of fun in class at the cliché, "the journey *is* the destination," but I probably wasn't fully clear. I remain enough of a traditional Christian to believe in some final, eschatological denouement of human history, some ultimate revelation of God's absolute truth, if you will. In which case we will, in a sense, truly *reach* the destination, and not simply grope wildly forever in the darkness. On the other hand, my own view of this destination is that it is the inexhaustible ecstasy of divine love, which the saints will spend all of eternity enjoying and growing in. In short, a "destination" or "endpoint" which is itself an infinite "journey" in, and to, and with God. On this, see *The End for Which God Created the World* by Jonathan Edwards.

Peace,

RBS

SUBJECT: RELATIVISM AND THE LOSS OF FAITH

Dr. Steele,

I have heard you speak around campus during my three years here at SPU. I was quite interested to learn that you had studied under Henri Nouwen, one of my favorites.[4] I am writing you today because I am interested in a possible dialogue about faith in our modern world.

My drive to initiate this sort of correspondence comes from deep crises within my very being. To give you a very brief explanation of myself, I am a pre-med SPU junior who has wanted to be some form of a minister—living life for Christ—since about 9th grade. Change really started when I came back from my four months in Europe last summer. I had lived mostly in Spain studying Spanish in a local program.

When I arrived back in the US, I plunged right into my usual ministry-oriented lifestyle. However, things seemed strangely empty and cynical. I was working as a counselor at a Christian camp when truth became relative to me. Since then, I have battled with faith v. unbelief and experienced a great emptiness that I never thought myself vulnerable to. I even started living wildly by experimenting for the first time with "sex and drugs and rock-n-roll." I do not understand my actions, yet I trace them back to my spiritual conflicts. Since these times I have gone to counselors, pastors and the like seeking help. I have toned down my "wild living," but this emptiness is still there.

Thoughts that I would like to discuss via email or otherwise pertain to my personal experience: Truth seems so relative when looking through the eyes of various cultures. How do we balance a faith in God (which is all I really want) with the knowledge that seems to show people as nothing more than fickle, conditioned members of a swaying society?

Thank you for your time in reading about my confusion and concerns. I have always prided myself on being able to have a ready answer for the hope that lies within me regarding Christ, and I guess that I want that back.

Alan

Dear Alan,

Thank you for writing. I would be happy to have a dialogue with you, although my time is quite limited for the next few months, and I may not be able to answer your questions or reply to your opinions in quite the depth and with quite the frequency they clearly deserve. But I will do my best.

First, at those times when the questions with which you are wrestling strike me with peculiar force (as they often have in the past, and sometimes still do), I take comfort in remembering that for Christianity, "truth" has a human face. In the last analysis, it is not a set of propositions (though it *includes* some of those) but rather a Person.

Now there are inexhaustible depths of mystery in every person, including—and indeed, most especially—Jesus Christ. Therefore one must never expect to fully "understand" any person, particularly Christ. Or rather, one's understanding of a person is always *growing,* but never *definitive* and *unrevisable.* Human communion is like an asymptote on a graph: one is always approaching it, but one never quite arrives.[5]

Such a model will be very frustrating if you are one of those people who think of "truth," particularly divine truth, as a set of demonstrable propositions that one is supposed to assert proudly and defend staunchly. Because it means that you will never "fully" know the truth of God. On the other hand, it at least turns the process of learning the truth into a grand adventure, a lifelong pilgrimage, a covenant partnership, and a love affair—as opposed, say, to the rather cold business of learning a batch of official formulas. Moreover, it allows room for new discoveries, occasional revisions, and ever-wider perspectives, without, however, forcing you to make a wholesale denial of all your previous insights every time you attain a new one.

Let me offer an analogy: I've been married now for over 20 years. My wife and I know each other very well. We have shared many joys and sorrows over the years. We can often complete each other's sentences. And we know most of each other's hot buttons. Yet we both continue to grow and change, and therefore we both continue to surprise each other at times. And precisely *because* we continue to surprise each other occasionally, our marriage retains something of its original zest and adventurousness. Of course, like all analogies, this one limps a bit. The relationship between God and the Christian is not the same as the relationship between husband and wife, because God does not "grow and change." But the Christian does, and therefore her comprehension of God will, too. Yet that does not imply that everything she believed at earlier stages of her spiritual life is invalidated every time she sees some new element of the truth; it only means that the older *formulation* must be modified and nuanced. The name for the ongoing process of reformulating one's theological ideas in light of one's growing knowledge and wisdom is not vertiginous relativism. It is spiritual maturation.

There is, of course, still need and plenty of room in this model for *truth claims*. For example, if one *absolutely* denied that *in any sense* the man Jesus of Nazareth had been restored to new and eternal life after his grisly death, one would have given up an essential element of the faith. But the real tragedy of such a denial is not that one thereby falls into "unbelief," but rather that one thereby disqualifies oneself from the possibility of any further comradeship with the living Lord. On the other hand, one *can* give up certain ways of formulating or interpreting the creedal proposition that Christ has been raised from the dead without giving up the proposition itself. (That is why the most useful and enduring creeds are always the ones that establish wide boundaries within which fruitful theological debate can proceed, not those which are so narrow and so overly precise that "revision" is impossible and whose eventual obsolescence is therefore virtually certain.)

Let me close with a conjecture: I suspect that the "emptiness and unbelief" you are feeling is due, not to the instability of your faith, but rather to the inadequacy of your *epistemology.* By that I mean, I think you may be laboring under an overly constrictive understanding of what "knowing the truth" is, and therefore have no good way to account for the Truth that you have actually come to know. The problem is not that people are "unstable" (that's surely no news!), or that the formulations of truth which suit one generation or culture prove inadequate to another generation or culture (that's not news either). The problem is that the "truth" which God has revealed to us in Christ is not finally a set of ideas to be debated, defended, and refuted, but rather a Person to be encountered and followed.

Best wishes,

RBS

NOTES

1 I borrow this term from James Wm. McClendon, Jr. and James M. Smith, *Convictions: Defusing Religious Relativism* (Valley Forge, PA: Trinity Press International, 1994), and much in my account of soft perspectivism is indebted to that work. We must distinguish *soft* perspectivism from *hard* perspectivism, which is simply another term for relativism.

2 Cf. Eric Hoffer, *The True Believer: Thoughts on the Nature of Mass Movements* (New York: Harper, 1951).

3 My meaning would have been clearer, or at least closer to the conventional nomenclature of the leading theoreticians of postmodernism, if I had used the word "constructed" instead of the word "created" throughout.

4 I attended Yale Divinity School from 1974 to 1978, when Fr. Nouwen was on the faculty.

5 I first heard this striking and useful analogy from Dr. Robert Masson, Professor of Theology at Marquette University, where I did my graduate work. He, in turn, ascribes it to Karl Rahner.

CHAPTER 7

ENCOUNTERING GOD IN WORSHIP

Worship is central to the Christian life. It is how we direct our minds and hearts toward God. I would like us to think about worship—about the God we worship and how to worship God rightly. I find three misconceptions about worship among evangelicals today.

The first is purely semantic. Some tend to equate "worship" with singing, and especially with singing contemporary praise songs. This doesn't mean that, when they're in church or chapel, they don't readily join in other liturgical actions and gestures. They do. They cheerfully recite the written prayers, listen attentively to the reading of Scripture and the preaching of sermons, and gladly participate in the Lord's Supper and other rituals, providing they aren't too formal. Yet they don't think of these other things as worship. Recently one of our campus ministers announced: "Next Tuesday morning we'll have an all-worship chapel service." How odd! What else would we be doing in chapel? But the students understood her perfectly. She was promising them fifty minutes of non-stop singing.

To correct this mistake, let's look at the word "worship," which comes from the Old English word *weorthscipe*, an act of acknowledging someone's worth or value and treating her accordingly. Thus, in the wedding liturgies found in older English prayer books, each partner would say to the other: "With my body, I thee worship."[1] They were promising to respect one another and to honor the intimate covenant between them. So too, when Christians worship *God*, we acknowledge that God is supremely good and absolutely sovereign. Everything we do when we enter into God's presence is worship—singing, yes, but also listening to God's word, reciting prayers and psalms, offering our tithes and talents, receiving the sacraments, and enjoying Christian fellowship.

The second problem is more difficult to correct, because it's hard for many people to see that it really *is* a problem. This is what I call "liturgical subjectivism," the attitude that the outward forms of Christian worship exist primarily to induce some inward attitude or experience. We often assume that what matters spiritually is what goes on "in the heart." We measure the depth of our faith by the intensity of our religious emotions, and regard anything that helps to arouse a devotional mood as spiritually enriching, and we often associate religious sincerity with spontaneity in action and gesture—the freedom to raise our hands to the skies (or not), to fall on our knees (or not), to dance in the aisles (or not), to speak in tongues (or not), as the Spirit leads. The idea that the church has anything to say about what is or isn't appropriate in liturgical settings strikes some as oppressive. Ancient customs, conventional proprieties, and carefully choreographed ceremonies generally seem to be stodgy and contrived.

Now, as a Wesleyan, I place great stock in "heart religion," and believe that emotion has an important place in the Christian faith. But I also know that when the Bible speaks of the "heart," it refers not just to our passing emotions, but to the self in its wholeness, that deep center of the personality where affect, intellect, and will coalesce.[2] Those who have a "heart" for God are not those who are religiously excitable, but those who are truly responsive to God. And responsiveness to God is wrought in us by the secret action of God's Spirit, as mediated through the community of faith and its practices, customs, rituals, and disciplines. Faith *is* a highly refined form of subjectivity, and worship *does* play a crucial role in shaping, modulating, and focusing our faith. But that doesn't mean that faith consists of gusts of pious emotion or that the chief aim of worship is to induce them. Worship is a means of grace, and grace may be mediated to us in worship even when we're not conscious of it. We can be motivated by liturgy, even when we're not obviously "moved" by it. We can be spiritually and morally transformed by divine grace, even when we're not psychologically stimulated in any overt way by ritual.

This brings me to a third problem. Some evangelicals believe that we are saved by faith alone, and contribute nothing to our salvation by our pious exercises and charitable deeds. As Paul says, "A person is justified not by the works of the law but through faith in Jesus Christ" (Galatians 2:16). Now, as long as we take this verse as a corrective to works-righteousness and self-salvation, all is well. But we must be careful. For strictly speaking, it isn't *our faith* that rescues us from the law of sin and death. It is *God's grace*, manifest in the life, death, and resurrection of Jesus Christ. Faith is our grateful response to God's work on our behalf, and, as we have noted, even that is awakened in us by the Holy Spirit. Hence, another Pauline verse is a more exact rendering of things: "*By* grace you have been saved *through* faith, and this is not your own doing; it is the gift of God—not the result of works, so that no one may boast" (Ephesians 2:8–9, emphasis added). The problem with saying we are saved *by* faith, rather than saying we are saved *by* grace *through* faith, is that it can lead to the very mistake it is supposed to correct. It can throw us back on our own feeble resources by causing us to fix our attention on our own subjective state.

If we are saved by grace through faith, then worship isn't just our subjective celebration of salvation; it's also our objective appropriation of it. These two poles must be kept in balance. We've already seen the danger of tilting too far toward subjectivism, which trivializes the *act* of worship by turning into a form of pious entertainment aimed at inducing some kind of "religious experience" in us. But liturgical objectivism—pomp, fussiness, empty ceremonialism, and, at its outer reaches, rank superstition—is just as dangerous. For that trivializes the *object* of worship. Divine grace, which worship communicates, is turned into a rarefied spiritual "stuff," which we consume. To strike the proper balance, we must remember that worship is a divinely instituted vehicle through which we encounter a gracious, personal God. In worship, the gospel of divine love is both proclaimed to the faithful and performed by them. Liturgy isn't show-and-tell—even though God's mighty acts of salvation are both "shown" in the sacraments and "told" in the sermon.

Neither is it white magic—even though something wonderful and mysterious "happens" there: Christ becomes present to, in, among, and for his people.

One cautionary note: Thinking theologically about Christian worship is not the same as worshipping. Let's not waste Sunday mornings engaging in highbrow critiques of the sermon and the liturgy. The sanctuary isn't a classroom, and when we enter it, we do so not primarily as students of theology, but as servants of God.

SUBJECT: THE ARTS IN WORSHIP

Dr. Steele,

I have a couple of questions for you. First, in class we were talking about using the arts as a medium to God. You said that one needs to find the balance so we don't start worshipping the medium. My question is how does one find a practical way of doing so? The reason I ask is that I work very closely with the youth of our church and see that this is a problem when it comes time to have a prayer meeting. When there is no music it seems like they can't pray, but when there is then they are more likely to.

Second, it seems as though Zwingli[3] is separating and limiting worship in meeting God through the church only. The reason I say this is because he doesn't throw out the arts entirely, but only prohibits their use in church. If our whole life is to be worship, and if music is not a means to God, then it seems as though going to a concert is all done for selfish reasons. My question is, did Zwingli believe that the arts in no way reflect God?

Kenneth

Good morning, Kenneth!

Thanks for your post, and for your very penetrating questions. Let me answer them in turn. As to your first, let me begin by commending you for being so observant. The capacity to notice such things is one of the key gifts of a genuine pastor. But from what you have said, I am not sure you really have a problem. If music draws your kids into prayer more successfully than silence, then by all means use music. It is serving as a medium for worship, not the object of worship, and that is how it should be. The key thing is to be sure they are worshipping God through the music, not making the enjoyment of the music an end in itself. If they are making the enjoyment of the music an end in itself, then you do, indeed, have a problem on your hands. There are several things you might try: You might try varying the music you play: different styles, tempos, volumes, etc. If you want to encourage them to be really quiet, that is, to enter God in the silence, you might work up to it (or down to it) gradually. From loud, thumping, attention-getting songs, to slower and softer ones. And see what happens. You might also try asking the kids to describe to you what effect music has on their prayer life, what emotions it arouses in them, how it helps them focus on God, what they think about, etc. Don't expect very profound or extensive or self-revealing answers at first. Those sorts of questions require a level of reflectiveness that teenagers don't always have, although it is precisely by making them think about such questions that teenagers acquire the reflectiveness that you want them to have. Let me know how things go on your pastoral experiments. I'm exceedingly interested in these matters!

Regarding your second question, I don't think Zwingli would necessarily deny your claim that all of life should be worship, although I'm not sure he would be inclined to put it quite that way. I suspect he would be more prone to say that all of life should be obedient to God's will. Certainly all of life should be lived in a prayerful and God-glorifying spirit. But Zwingli, I think, would limit the use of the term "worship" to what is done in church (and perhaps also to our daily private devotions), and it is there that he thinks that all sensuous distractions and temptations to idolatry and superstition must be removed. For Zwingli, there is nothing wrong with enjoying earthly beauty, as long as one does not confuse it with the holy gospel. The question is whether the enjoyment of earthly beauty can draw one into deeper contemplation of, and into more earnest obedience to, the holy gospel. Zwingli thinks not. Most of us, I suspect, would think so.

RBS

SUBJECT: SACRAMENTAL GRACE

Dr. Steele:

I had a quick question for you. What was the purpose
of grace before Luther's time? As far as I understand,
the purpose of grace is to reconcile people to God. Am
I wrong in thinking that? If the purpose of grace is to
reconcile people to God, then why would grace ever need
to be dispensed through things? I can understand the
justification of God dispensing his grace through people,
even though I don't believe it, but it doesn't make sense
through things. Where did the idea come from that God's
grace, namely Christ, could or would even need to reside
in things or objects? Maybe I don't fully understand the
purpose of grace before Luther's time. Any thoughts?

Jesse

Dear Jesse:

I think it is fair to say that the broad consensus among
Christian theologians, East and West, throughout most of the
history of the church, would be that "grace" is the name we
give to God's reconciling love for sinful humanity. But from
there the problems proliferate. To name only two of the major
ones:

First, *on whom* is grace bestowed? Is it ultimately bestowed
on everyone? (That is, is hell ultimately empty?) Or is
grace offered to everyone, but bestowed only on those who
voluntarily "accept" it? Or is it both offered to and bestowed

upon only a minority of people, namely "the elect"? All three of those suggestions have been made by different theologians, based upon different proof texts from Scripture and different arguments about the nature of God.

Second, *how* is grace bestowed? Only through preaching? (In which case there is no real need for sacraments, and preaching becomes the sole means of grace.) Or through other means, such as rituals, ceremonies, spiritual disciplines, etc. Here the consensus, at least for the first fifteen centuries of Christian history, is a bit clearer. Most Christians have said that there are various means of grace, certainly including those that were explicitly authorized by the Lord, namely baptism and the Eucharist. Now, if sacraments are means of grace, and if sacraments include some "visible sign" (water in the case of baptism, bread and wine in the case of the Eucharist, oil in the case of anointing, the exchange of rings in the case of marriage, etc.), then what role does the sign itself play in the transmission of grace? You can't have a sacrament without the sign, so presumably the sign is necessary. But why and how is it necessary? One answer that seemed plausible to Christians who were steeped in Greek metaphysics, no less than the biblical message, was that grace was to be understood "ontologically," i.e., as some sort of thing or substance that inhered somehow in whatever was consecrated to God and/or appointed by God for the furtherance of his holy and gracious purposes.

Aside from this somewhat formal, theological motive for conceptualizing grace ontologically, there were more "popular" (but no less powerful) motives operating toward the same end. For example, in the days when Christians were being martyred, their friends were sometime responsible for disposing of the bodies. How do you treat the corpse of someone who has died for the faith and is presumably now in glory? Presumably with the greatest respect and reverence! And how do you tend their grave? Again, with the utmost diligence! It's not hard to understand, therefore, why "relics" came to be venerated and burial sites came to be places of pilgrimage. They were "things" with which grace was associated, "objects" whose holiness was palpable to those who remembered or understood the witness of the holy person himself or herself.

RBS

SUBJECT: THE PRESENCE OF CHRIST IN COMMUNION

Dr. Steele,

Perhaps I am failing in my effort to put myself in the spirit of the time of the Reformation in order to understand where the Reformers were coming from and what motivated them, but it seems trifling to me that the main issue dividing Protestants during the time of Calvin was the manner in which Christ was present in communion. González comments that this "should not have been an insurmountable obstacle to Protestant unity."[4] It was though, and it seems that the followers of Luther and Calvin only promoted disunity. Would it be fair to argue that at this point the original intent of the Reformation was lost and the birth of what can now be seen as a continual fracturing of the church through denominational splits and disagreements came to be? Or is it better to say that this was instead a rather typical outcome of such a reform movement? Any insight would be greatly appreciated! Thanks!

Sharon

Dear Sharon,

What wonderfully penetrating questions you ask! And I assure you that even if you may, in some respects, be "failing to put yourself in the spirit of the time of the Reformation," the very fact that you are making so heroic an effort to do so is exceedingly admirable. Such is the difficulty of historical inquiry, that such mistakes are frequent and inevitable, even for the most learned and careful scholars! Indeed, the passage you quote from González suggests that on this issue of the Lord's Supper, even he has failed to be adequately sympathetic to the concerns of the sixteenth century.

From our vantage point it is indeed difficult not to think that the dispute between the Lutherans and the Reformed over how Christ is "present" in the Eucharist was "trifling." (And quite aside from the Lord's obvious desire for unity among *all* his followers, it seems astounding to us that the disagreement over this issue was allowed to prevent the Protestants of Saxony and Switzerland from achieving a political alliance that would have been extremely advantageous to both.) Yet in making a statement about what "should not have happened," González has ceased speaking as an objective historian (if there is such a thing) and has made an evaluative statement that reveals the prejudices of *our* time. Ours is a "pluralistic" and "relativistic" age, whereas the sixteenth century was a "dogmatic" age. Unlike ourselves, the people of that time were fiercely passionate about theological "truth," believed implicitly that the sources at their disposal ("Scripture alone," said the Protestants; "Scripture and church tradition," said the Catholics) enabled them to know precisely what that truth was, and therefore concluded that any disagreement over truth was caused by the perversity of their adversaries. Moreover, they regarded the Eucharist not as a trifling matter, but as a matter of absolutely central importance to Christianity, for they regarded it as the ceremony which the Lord himself had commissioned his followers to observe in order to receive the benefits of his atoning work. Paradoxically, the reason the disagreements between Lutherans and Zwinglians (and Catholics and Anglicans) about how to understand the Lord's Supper were so bitter is precisely that they all shared the fundamental presupposition that in it God's grace is (somehow) symbolized and made effectual. Put sharply, the Lord's Supper was regarded as a microcosm of the whole "economy of salvation," and the disagreements over the microcosm were as intense as they were because they reflected disagreements over the macrocosm. Whether that presupposition is correct or not is, of course, a theological question, not a historical one.

RBS

SUBJECT: SACRAMENTS

Hi Dr. Steele,

I had many questions during our session today that kept
coming up in my mind.[5] How do you, as a Protestant,
handle the loss of tradition and holiness in the
sacraments? Being raised in a non-denominational church,
I never had a holy view of communion. It was simply
something you did in church during the first of the month.
However, as I have actively claimed my walk with Christ
the past year, communion is amazing. Delving into church
history, there is so much about our faith that is not taught
in the church body. Now that I have a hunger for God's
word, questions keep coming into my head about certain
aspects of this world. I finally understand what people
mean when they say, "Ignorance is bliss." Questions of
theology rack your brain with things you never thought
you'd be concerned about!

When we discussed sacramental grace, I think I saw the
picture but would like to rephrase it, just to make sure
I have the concept figured out. The Medievals had it
backwards. They wished to use the sacrament for grace
instead of Christ. They saw the sacraments as means of
grace for the forgiveness of their sins: sacrament → me
→ grace. Instead, we should love God in realization of
the great grace already given through Jesus Christ: Christ
→ grace → me → sacrament. Taking the sacrament with
joy, we see it as "a visible form of invisible grace."[6] Out
of the overflow of our heart, we do good works. We take
communion to represent His flesh and blood shed for us,

so that we may continue the journey of brokenness in this life. The Medievals were in some sense hypocrites, trying to fix the outside by painting it, instead of gutting it out and remodeling the inside. The sacrament wasn't bad; the state of their heart was, and how they viewed the sacrament was. Is that the point of Luther's criticisms?

Okay, just one more question. Is it wrong, being myself from Protestant background, to want to partake in a church body that focuses more on sacraments? The more I learn about church history and theology and fall in love with our Maker, the more I want to find a church which represents a more traditional path and which follows the liturgical calendar more. I want to wash people's feet, have Ash Wednesday services, and celebrate the Stations of the Cross. When you commented on not being able to bow to "the bread in the globe,"[7] I stopped and contemplated if I could. Over the past year, I've read numerous works of theology stemming from Mother Teresa and Dietrich Bonhoeffer to Richard Foster, Catherine of Genoa, and Marvin Olasky. The thought of giving the leftover sacrament to the sick in the community is beautiful. Jesus' face is beautiful and being able to give a blessed sacrament on behalf of the Healer would be amazing. It is unique, holy, and wonderful. I know you know that you're not bowing to simply bread in a globe, but the Prince of Peace. He is the ultimate sacrifice, and we can remember Him in sacraments and baptism.

Ellen

Dear Ellen:

Thank you for your extremely thoughtful and thought-provoking message. Let me begin by saying how much I resonated personally with your comments about the effects that studying theology has had on you. Yes, there is a certain sadness that comes from losing one's spiritual "innocence." But the statement that "ignorance is bliss" is never made by the ignorant. For the ignorant don't know they are enjoying bliss, precisely because they are, well, ignorant. It is only those who, from the vantage point of spiritual maturity and intellectual sophistication, can look back on their former state with wistfulness and nostalgia. Yet I want to assure you that one of the unexpected dividends of the study of theology—if it is undergirded by a lively prayer life and active participation in the ministries of the church—is the ultimate dawning of what has sometimes been called a "second innocence." This is a simple, childlike delight in the truth of God—minus the naïveté and simplemindedness of the first state, but also minus the intellectual restlessness and uncertainty of the state you seem to be in now. So let me encourage you by saying that it seems to me that you are on exactly the right path as a young theologian, and that you are exactly where you belong on that path, given your age and level of experience. Hang in there, the wisdom and peace that come from long acquaintance with the deep things of God will come!

Now on to the particular matters that Friday's class raised in your mind: First, I must emphasize that it was largely because of my association with Roman Catholics that I have come to a much deeper appreciation of the sacraments than I had growing up in liberal Protestant churches. I participated almost daily in Henri Nouwen's afternoon Eucharist service at Yale Divinity School for two years in the mid-'70s, was a frequent visitor to a Trappist monastery in Dubuque, Iowa in the late '70s and early '80s, and went to a Jesuit graduate school (Marquette University) in the mid-to-late '80s. And I have studied Roman Catholic ecclesiology and sacramentalogy in some depth. My story about being unable to bow at solemn benediction was intended to show—and perhaps I should clarify this to the class—that my religious sensibilities were, at that time, in a state of flux. I understood perfectly what they were doing and why, and I deeply admired their fervent eucharistic piety, but somehow it just felt awkward and inappropriate to me to adore the reserved sacrament as it was carried past me. My theologically trained mind got the point, my ecumenically sensitive heart ached to share in the devotion, but my all-too-Protestant body was stuck. Yet the real value of that experience was that it revealed to me how deep our religious sensibilities can be—so deep that we are surprised at our own responses to new situations. But I will say that I am now much more sympathetic to the Catholic tendency to reverence the "reserved sacrament" than I am to the irreverent and supercilious way that many mainline Protestants deal with "the leftovers" after communion, and indeed, with the way they conduct the sacraments and other sacred rituals. Moreover, I crave to participate in a Christian community in which other ancient Christian rituals and ceremonies, like the ones you mention (foot-washing, imposition of the ashes, etc.) are performed with a sensitivity to the power and significance of the symbolism, and I am frustrated to be stuck in a congregation that just doesn't get this at all.

Second, I do not think it is the task of Christians in our time to judge the spiritual state of Christians of other times. To speak more plainly, I do not think that it is proper for us to accuse Catholics of the 15th and 16th century of hypocrisy, although I certainly do think it is proper for us to assess theologically their theory and practice of worship. That said, I would argue that the very strength of the Roman theory of the sacraments—namely that they are effective *ex opera operato*, as acts performed by duly commissioned officers of the church in obedience to divine command and in accordance with church law—is also its greatest weakness. This theory insists on the objective efficacy of the sacraments, and hence is particularly valuable in ensuring that they be accorded proper respect. But taken too far, it can lead to superstition and fanaticism, as if the sacraments were some kind of "white magic." The Protestant critique of the Catholic theory was plausible precisely because of the superstition to which it had given rise. But what the Reformers (not so much Luther, but certainly Zwingli) replaced it with had the opposite tendency, i.e., subjectivism. We Protestants tend to regard the sacraments as efficacious only to the degree that they trigger something in the hearts of the worshippers. The sacraments become something like audio-visual aids, teaching methods, reminders of bygone events, etc. We have demystified the sacraments, but in so doing we have grown disenchanted with ritual altogether. And such disenchantment can easily lead to a complete loss of faith in the Christ who makes himself present to us through his appointed "means of grace."

The truth of the matter, so it seems to me, is dialectical. That is, each side in this debate has a point that the other needs to hear if the divine truth, which is greater than either theory by itself, is to be apprehended by the church as a whole.

Best wishes,

RBS

NOTES

1 James F. White, *Introduction to Christian Worship* (Nashville: Abingdon Press, 1980), 25.

2 See R. C. Denton, "Heart," *The Interpreter's Dictionary of the Bible*, 4 vols. (Nashville and New York: Abingdon Press, 1962), 4:549f.

3 Ulrich Zwingli (1484–1531) established the Protestant Reformation in Switzerland. Like Martin Luther, whose reforming work in Germany preceded his by only a few years, he insisted that the Scriptures are the sole norm of Christian doctrine and that persons are justified by faith alone. He differed from Luther in regarding the sacraments only as "signs" of grace, rather than "means" of grace, and in refusing to permit the use of the visual arts (icons, statues, clerical vestments) and instrumental music in Christian worship

4 Justo L. González, *The Story of Christianity*, Volume 2: *The Reformation to the Present Day* (New York: HarperCollins Publishers, 1985), 69. This is a required text for my course on the Reformation.

5 Ellen was responding to one of the first lectures in my course on the Reformation, in which I had described the moral and sacramental theology of the late Middle Ages against which the early Protestant Reformers were reacting.

6 This succinct definition of a sacrament was proposed by Augustine of Hippo, which I quoted in my lecture.

7 Ellen is referring to a story I told in class about an experience I once had during an extended retreat at a Trappist monastery. The community celebrates "solemn benediction" on Friday afternoons, a ceremony in which the consecrated host is carried around the sanctuary in a crystal monstrance and reverenced by the congregation. As noted in my response to Ellen's letter, that was one devotional exercise that my ingrained Protestant religious sensibilities prevented me from participating in fully.

CHAPTER 8

FAITH
IN
PRACTICE

What is the proper relationship between "faith" and "good works"? This is a perennial question for Christians. Most of us would agree with the Pauline formula (discussed in the previous chapter) that we are saved by grace through faith—not by good works. But how are we to interpret it? Today we hear echoes of the "strict Lutheran" concern to ward off all forms of works-righteousness, the Reformed concern to "Christianize society," the Wesleyan concern for personal purity, and the Pentecostal concern for deeply felt and vibrantly expressed religious experience. Naturally, these themes amalgamate and cross-fertilize in complex ways.

Each of these "concerns" arose in response to a particular set of social and religious problems. (Luther was attacking the late medieval penitential system; the early Puritans were trying to build their "city on a hill;" and so forth.) But how do these different concerns relate—or *not* relate—to our contemporary situation. (Do we *really* need to share Luther's worry that people will try to earn their way into heaven? *Are* they trying? Or again: what happens when we try to "Christianize" a society where religious freedom is constitutionally guaranteed? Might we be violating the law of the land in our very attempt to honor the law of God? What then?)

The faith/works issue is a paradox—one of many that crop up in Christian theology. We know that we aren't saved by what we do, but by what Christ has done for us. We also know that what we do in obedience to God and in service to our neighbors matters—and matters ultimately. But here's the kicker: all efforts to explain how these statements can both be true seem to privilege one over the other. They tilt us toward antinomianism on the one hand or moralism on the other. What we say on paper doesn't live up to what we know in practice. And therefore, everything depends on seeing that if the faith/works paradox is to be resolved at all, it won't be resolved by the clever spinning of theories, but by the faithful living of the Christian life. Put differently, the analysis of moral theories is of value precisely because, but only to the extent that, it reveals the various ways we can go wrong in the day to day business of following Jesus. But going right in that business is not done in the classroom. It's done in the bedroom, the boardroom, and the dining room.

What questions arise when we study the various Christian "theories" of the faithful life and ask how the historical "concerns" listed above have been put into practice? Here's one: Does Paul's insistence that "there is no distinction [between Jew and Greek], since all have sinned and fall short of the glory of God" (Romans 3:22b–23) mean that "all sins are equal" in moral gravity? It may be that all *persons* stand in absolute need of God's grace; but does that imply that all *sins* are uniformly reprehensible in God's eyes? Yes, we should leave it to God to pass judgment on human beings; but mustn't we still learn how to distinguish between good and evil and how to analyze the ways in which various psycho-social motives, religious values, social customs, and government policies affect human lives? Here's another: Do we "sin" only when we, as individuals, knowingly and willfully violate the laws of God? Or are we also guilty before God when we participate in social structures that oppress people or damage the environment—even though there is no way to avoid participating in them? Here's a third: Do only those people who believe in Jesus Christ qualify for salvation? Can we really believe that the God who is revealed in Jesus would condemn Mahatma Gandhi to hell, or that the woman who rejects Christianity after being sexually abused by her pastor is morally equivalent in God's eyes to the genocidal war criminal?

Such questions are more than brain-teasers. They have a morally bracing effect on us when we apply them to ourselves. They help us see that it's just as Pharisaical for Christians to claim superiority to non-Christians on the basis of our orthodox beliefs as it is to do so on the basis of our unblemished conduct. That it's just as antinomian to assert that ax murder is as wrong as raiding the cookie jar as it is to assert that God's law is no longer binding on the followers of Christ. That being saved *from* the curse of the law is being saved *for* the care of the neighbor. That faith liberates us from guilt-ridden self-obsession *and* from irresponsible self-indulgence. That having a sensitive conscience means being fiercely introspective *and* blithely self-forgetful. That following Christ means being dedicated to good causes (even good *lost* causes) and yet confident in God's providence.

SUBJECT: NATURAL LAW

Dr. Steele,

God says that He will inscribe His law on the hearts of his people. Do nonbelievers really know—deep down—right and wrong? Has God embedded in our world certain "natural laws" whether or not they are accepted as secular law? I feel that Anne Frank's statement at the end of her diary, "I believe there is some good in all people," is not true. I used to agree with Anne, but the more I learn of the human psyche and hear of the Ted Bundys of this world, I truly don't think we all have a basic ground of what's evil. What's sin to a nonbeliever? Why try to be "good?" What is good if one does not know Christ? Do people like serial killers really have a conscience? Are these great tragedies (referring to those who have killed many) simply flukes in society? If natural laws do exist, how are they discerned? Who interprets? Should we try to implement natural laws in a pluralistic society? Deep down I think we should, but is it right to push personal convictions (that is, commands from Scripture and the Holy Spirit) on another?

Thank you,

Nadine

Hi Nadine,

Thanks for your profound and thought-provoking questions about natural law. Let me begin this response by saying that you should probably make a clearer conceptual distinction between natural law and original sin. That is, you should differentiate between our "natural" ability to comprehend the moral good and our inescapable (but in a sense unnatural) tendency to do the exact opposite. The reason this distinction is so crucial is that the former, though certainly impaired by the fall, has to be intact enough for us to be held morally accountable for our sins. There is no doubt that our moral sensibilities have been corrupted by original sin, and are further corrupted by every actual sin. But if our conscience is so blind that we simply cannot tell the difference between right and wrong, then we are either insane (and therefore innocent by reason of insanity) or morally equivalent to squirrels and turnips and sandstone (i.e., not accountable moral agents at all). However, to say that we must be able to *know* right from wrong does not imply that we have the ability to *will* the right consistently. The term "original sin" is the theological way of referring to our apparent inability to will the right consistently. Yet even that inability cannot be said to be "natural." For what is "salvation" but the restoration of the capacity to will what God wills us to will? Put differently, we can't say that human nature is *inherently* sinful, because then one of two theologically catastrophic consequences follow: Either Christ, being fully human, must be guilty of original and personal sin, in which case he can't be our savior, or we can't be saved from sin without ceasing to be fully human ourselves. Thus, Christianity insists that sin is that which God in Christ is in the process of eradicating from us, thus enabling us to become what he intended us to be, willingly obedient to and utterly in love with him.

Now, as to the question of serial killers, I'm not sure that a general explanation can be given for them, or even that we are in a position to know what to make of them. Where does the line between radical evil and utter insanity lie? God knows. And thank God that God knows, because we surely don't. Nor do I have any idea what to do with them: Life imprisonment seems almost too lenient. Capital punishment seems barbaric. Incarceration in a locked ward in an insane asylum presumes mental illness rather than moral culpability, which seems insufficient to the gravity of the case. But what else is there besides these three equally inadequate responses? On the other hand, the very inadequacy of the responses to radical evil and mental defect is itself a sign of our fallenness.

And as to how Christian moral standards should influence life in a secularized and pluralistic society, I would say this: The laws of the land should, to the extent possible, be a reflection of the public moral consensus. Now, we Christians can and should help to shape that consensus by lively participation in the political process. We cannot and should not presume to dictate the outcome of that process unilaterally. But we can and should demonstrate the intrinsic wisdom of our position by living according to God's standards, which are much higher than those of the state. In other words, the discrepancy between the "natural laws," which all reasonable and morally mature people should be expected to understand (plus the "positive laws" which follow from them), and the "divine laws" which we voluntarily take upon ourselves is great. But we need to see the discrepancy not just as a tragic and unavoidable necessity due to human fallenness, but also as a missionary opportunity, i.e., as an obligation which circumstance lays upon us to embody and proclaim the gospel.

Hope these quick reflections help. Thanks for raising such important questions.

RBS

SUBJECT: "BIGGER" AND "SMALLER" SINS

Dr. Steele:

The discussion on "bigger sins" was very interesting today. I suppose somewhere I had heard that "a sin is a sin." Your comment today that some sins are worse than others was really a surprise to me (for obvious reasons), but it definitely made me sit back and want to delve into Scripture for some answers. I have yet to do that, but am very curious about what I may find.

Does earthly sin relate to a heavenly scale in any way? That question popped into my mind when you spoke of different levels of sin. It seems to me when studying the sacraments and different grace theories, I start to question my own salvation. I know it is secure in the name of Jesus and I am certain of it, but when I look throughout history at the different practices in order to attain grace and merit in the eyes of the Lord, I start to question if at the judgment seat we will really be seen through the eyes of Jesus.

Ellen

Dear Ellen:

Protestants tend to emphasize verses such as, "All have sinned and fall short of the glory of God" (Romans 3:23) and "There is no one who is righteous, not even one" (Romans 3:10) in order to focus our attention on the *absolute* need of all persons for unmerited divine grace. I am in deep sympathy with this strategy, and fully aware that the problem with the characteristically Catholic way of trying to determine which sins are "more" and "less" severe than others is that it tempts us to think there are greater and lesser degrees of need for divine grace. No, all of us need grace, all the time. But the problem with the Protestant tendency to regard all sins as "equal" (in God's eyes?) is that it can tempt us to think that ethical analysis of human conduct, socio-political institutions, economic systems, etc. is unnecessary. And that, I think, is a formula for moral disaster on an individual level and for grave injustice on a social level. My neighbor's welfare is a matter of great moral and spiritual significance—and some sins against my neighbor are obviously worse than others. If I think that all sins are equally "severe" in God's eyes, I can fall into the mistake of thinking that the "sin" of a poor man who steals a loaf of bread to feed his starving family is identical in severity to the sin of the people who profit from a system that allows babies to starve and causes frantic parents to steal.

RBS

* * * * *

Dr. Steele:

This email is written concerning the conversation that we had in class about how the church viewed some sins as greater than others. I of course realize that there are greater consequences for some of the sins that are committed. But 1 John 5:16–20 in particular speaks of sin that leads to death and sin that does not lead to death. In the context, the sin that leads to death is repetitive intentional sin. Then there is unintentional sin that does not lead to death, but Revelation 21:8 makes it clear that all liars will have their place in the lake of burning sulfur and will suffer the "second death." So even the "little white lies" that we tell intentionally are viewed by the Lord God as the same as any other intentional habitual sin.

Also you stated that in James there was scripture that gave credence to confession of sins to elders. I looked in the book of James and the closest thing to this that I could find was 5:13–16. These scriptures speak of elders and other righteous believers praying for one another, the sick in particular. It also speaks of confession of sins to one another and emphasizes how the Lord was the one who would heal them and forgive them of their sins. I was just trying to get clarity on if this was the correct scripture that you were referring to.

Anthony

Dear Anthony:

Most of what I would say in response to these very pertinent questions I have already said in response to Ellen's similar ones. I would only add that when theologizing, it is not sufficient simply to *cite* verses from Scripture. One must *interpret* them. And interpretations are always shaped by the pastoral problems faced by the church at any given time and place. (Scripture itself works this way: many of the authors of the biblical books wrote to address particular social, cultural, and religious situations faced by their original audience, and part of the task of understanding the Bible is attempting to reconstruct that setting.) Now the doctrine of sin, as preached by the church at a given time and place, must be articulated with sensitivity to the particular way in which people of that time and place are sinning, and the particular way they are trying (as all people do) to minimize their sinfulness in their own eyes. The Protestant claim that all sins, including seemingly minor ones, place the sinner in need of divine grace was articulated at a time when people were in the habit of focusing on the relative severity of different sins, rather than on the absolute need for God's pardon. But that claim is itself susceptible to gross distortion if it prevents us from taking into consideration the effects of our actions on our neighbor. For our neighbor's welfare is *always* our business: we *are* our brother's keeper. Thus, to use your example, I make no bones about contending that, morally and theologically, the "little white lie" that a person tells his diet counselor about his caloric intake for a given week is significantly different from the "big lie" that the Nazis told the German people about the way that Jews were corrupting their nation. If that were not so, we could not reasonably regard God as just. That God's justice may surpass human reason is not in question; but it certainly cannot fall below that level.

RBS

* * * * *

Dear Dr. Steele:

In this discussion of the various levels of sin, I am reminded of what my Christian Scriptures professor said during a lecture about the same topic. He said it is silly to proclaim that sins are all equal, that a little white lie is the same as murder in the eyes of the Lord. However, he said, though all *sin* may not be equal in God's eyes, all *forgiveness* is equal. God's grace and the sacrifice of Christ cover all sins equally and wipe them away if the sinner is truly repentant. What did the medieval church and the reformers think about that idea?

George

Dear George:

Thanks for this delightful post. I think your Christian Scriptures professor was exactly right. Some of the Reformers might have blanched at the idea that sins differ in severity—and if so, I think they would have been wrong. But most of them surely would have agreed that all forgiveness is absolute (and therefore "equal") to those who repent. The Medievals presumably would have said that sins differ in severity, but would also have agreed that ultimate forgiveness is "equal," although the amount of penance done before such forgiveness could be secured would have differed in proportion to the severity of the sin.

RBS

* * * * *

Dear Dr. Steele:

I want to go back to our discussion about how different sins have different consequences. I remember someone saying something along the lines that sins have different consequences, but are basically the same as far as "badness" goes. (I'm now wishing I had written this back when we talked about this, because now I think I'm getting it all wrong.) I've kind of thought of it as almost opposite if that. I always thought that sins had an equal consequence but that there were greater and lesser evils. It seems that, from what little I know, any sin committed causes you to be unworthy of salvation and in need of grace. Thus, "all have sinned and fall short of the glory of

God" (Romans 3:23) So spiritually, every sin does have the same consequence. Where I can see how sins would have different consequences is what happens here on earth. Like if I sin by killing someone, I'll obviously have to face more consequences in this life than I would if I had an impure thought. Are those two sins equal? I would say no, but each one still has the same spiritual consequences, that without Christ I am separated from God. I have more thoughts on that, but I'm one of those cursed people that can't put thoughts into words to save my life.

Matt

Dear Matt:

In saying that some sins are "worse" than others, I am making an ethical and a theological claim, but not one that I would want to try to translate into bookkeeping terms. By that I mean, I don't like the idea of supposing that God's way of judging us for, punishing us for, and/or redeeming us from our sins is quantifiable according to any reliable scheme of human reckoning. Thus, I am perfectly willing to say that murder is a far greater evil than stealing a cookie from the cookie jar. And it would be hard for me to respect and worship a God whom I believed to think otherwise, for such a God would not be operating according to any set of moral principles that I would be able to regard as just and rational. That does not mean, of course, that God's justice does not *transcend* mine. Surely it does. It had better! But it can't sink *below* mine. It had better not! Nor does it mean that the way in which God treats sinners is directly analogous to the way in which earthly judges mete out punishments for breaking the law (e.g., thirty days in jail for drinking while intoxicated, twenty years to life for murder, etc.) And, moreover, God knows *all* the extenuating circumstances for *all* sins, and looks upon the sinner's heart (i.e., his motives, intentions, etc.). So perhaps at times he reckons some sins that would seem worse to us as being of lesser gravity than others that might seem trivial to us. I'm willing to allow for that possibility. What I'm not willing to do is to suppose that God's justice is either trivial or arbitrary, as the statement that "all sins are equal" really ends up implying.

RBS

All SPU students take a vertically tiered triad of "University Foundations" courses. Freshmen take "Christian Formation." Sophomores take "Christian Scriptures." As juniors or seniors, they take "Christian Theology." Both of the posts under this subject heading were sent, independently of each other, in response to a particularly lively classroom conversation in the freshman course. With both authors' permission, I sent their posts, together with my answer, to the whole class. Several additional, and very thoughtful, student posts followed. I have omitted these for reasons of space, but I regret doing so, since their inclusion would have demonstrated that in many email conversations I do not have, or need to have, the last word.

SUBJECT: FAITH AND WEALTH

Dr. Steele,

I am writing regarding the class discussion that took place today regarding money. I do not agree with everything that you said. You did make a few good points that I do agree with, but I think that you are missing the main point.

The point you attempted to make regarding Christian churches that teach prosperity as a means of justifying their own selfishness was out of line. That is not even close to the actual truth. Those churches teach that God wants to bless and prosper his children because that is the truth. God does want to bless us and prosper us. I am not saying that we should let money be our main concern and let it control our lives. I agree with you on that. It is wrong to hoard your wealth. But merely having wealth is not wrong. It is what you do with it that makes it wrong. So often people try to justify their lack by saying that God does not want his people to have riches. That is not true. Look at many of the biblical characters. Abraham was a very wealthy man. God gave him all that wealth. It was what he did with it that made him so great. He wasn't selfish about what he had. That is the attitude that God wants for us. Jesus was not poor either. Look at his family. His father was a carpenter. That was a very wealthy job in that period. You also brought up the point of the first beatitude in Luke 6:20, which says, "Blessed are the poor, for yours is the kingdom of heaven," when in fact that is not the meaning of that verse at all. Matthew 5:3 says, "Blessed are the poor in spirit, for theirs is the kingdom of heaven." This verse does not relate to material wealth at all. In fact its meaning has to do with humility, not wealth.

I do agree with you in that Christians should give to those less fortunate than themselves because that is what God commands us to do. One thing that some people get wrong is that Jesus taught specifically against wealth. That is not true, either. Jesus taught against the love of money, not merely having it. There is quite a difference there. It is true that the love of money is wrong, and it can lead to sin. We shouldn't let our wealth control our entire lives and interfere in our relationship with God. That is where money becomes a sin. I hope you understand what I am trying to say. It took me a while to find the words to express what I was feeling in class. I could not explain it then, but I think this is what I am trying to say.

Lena

Dr. Steele,

I was having some personal time today with God, and He showed me something that made me think about part of our discussion in class today. I was reading in *My Utmost for His Highest* by Oswald Chambers. He makes the statement: "To choose to suffer means that there is something wrong. To choose God's will, even if it means suffering, is a very different thing. No healthy saint ever chooses suffering; he chooses God's will, as Jesus did, whether it means suffering or not." This made me think about what we were saying. God puts us where he wants us, and if it is His will, suffering will or will not come our way. We don't always know why we have to suffer, but God's greater plan does know the reason. That is where faith comes in. We have to trust that God really does know what he is doing, even if we don't understand. Also, some suffering comes from the sinfulness of this world. Bad things do happen to good people, and a lot of it is because of the sin that we chose as humans. But then God can work through those situations for His good. Later he says, "God puts His saints where they will glorify Him, and we are no judges at all of where that is." This just all really made think and gave me some clear answers to what we were talking about.

Joyce

Dear Lena and Joyce (and Class):

Thank you for your very thoughtful comments on yesterday's class. I'm afraid that I find myself in considerable disagreement with Lena's reading of the New Testament's teachings on wealth, and in particular with her assumption that Matthew 5:3 corrects Luke 6:20. For one thing, there is widespread agreement among Gospel scholars that Luke's version of the Beatitudes is probably closer to Jesus' original words, and that in "editing" Jesus' teachings, Matthew "spiritualized" the meaning. But that takes us into very complicated questions of biblical interpretation, which had better be left until UFDN 2000.

Here I will content myself by quoting the full text of blessings and parallel woes from Luke 6:20–26, which leaves no doubt that the Lukan Jesus is particularly harsh on those who are fortunately placed in this age, and proclaims a great reversal of fortunes in the age to come: "Blessed are you who are poor, for yours is the kingdom of God. Blessed are you who are hungry now, for you will be filled. Blessed are you who weep now, for you will laugh. Blessed are you when people hate you, and then they exclude you, revile you, and defame you on account of the Son of Man. Rejoice in that day and leap for joy, for surely your reward is great in heaven; for that is what their ancestors did to the prophets. But woe to you who are rich, for you have received your consolation. Woe to you who are full now, for you will be hungry. Woe to you who are laughing now, for you will mourn and weep. Woe to you when all speak well of you, for that is what their ancestors did to the false prophets." Jesus is blessing those who endure real poverty, real hunger, real grief, and real persecution, and bringing judgment upon those who complacently enjoy real wealth, real luxury, real frivolity, and real popularity. For corroborating evidence, see Jesus' parable of the rich man and Lazarus (Luke 16:19–31) and the story of the rich ruler (Luke 18:18–30).

Furthermore, the idea that carpentry was a highly lucrative job in first century Palestine is simply wrong. It was, perhaps, more lucrative than shepherding and farm labor, and under the Herods, who were famous for their monumental architectural projects, it seems plausible that skilled carpenters were in great demand. So we need not suppose that Jesus grew up dirt poor. But there is absolutely nothing to suppose that the Son of Man, who "had nowhere to lay his head" (Luke 9:58), was in any sense wealthy.

All this does not mean, however, that the New Testament simply equates righteousness with poverty and misfortune, and sinfulness with having possessions or enjoying health and worldly happiness. Here, Lena seems to me to be on the right track. We cannot downplay the goodness of God's creation, and therefore we need not imagine that God forbids us to take pleasure in it. Moreover, the NT bids us to share our blessings with the hungry, the sick, the naked, and the imprisoned (see Matthew 25). This presupposes that God wants people's basic creaturely needs to be met. And the Old Testament, especially prophets such as Amos and Isaiah, warns us in no uncertain terms that God stands in severe judgment of any socio-economic system that denies people what they need to survive: food, shelter, clothing, employment, etc. If my "hoarding" the goods of this life means that my neighbor suffers want, then I am sinning. And if the system enables the few to get rich while the many suffer want, then the whole system is at odds with God's will.

As to Joyce's comments, here I find myself in considerable agreement. The Bible teaches, on the one hand, that there is a moral order according to which prudent living and hard work generally promote one's own, as well as one's neighbor's flourishing, whereas foolishness, self-indulgence, and laziness generally lead to misfortune for oneself and probably misfortune for others, too. On the other hand, the Bible cautions us against taking that idea too far. It is flatly wrong to assume that simply because one is suffering, one must have been sinning. That is one of the key points of the book of Job in the OT, as well as the NT story of the healing of the man born blind (John 9:1–41). Suffering as such is not a good thing, so that it is not to be willed directly. But by the same token, much good can come out of suffering (see Rom. 5:1–5), and much suffering can come to those who do good in an evil world (e.g., prophets and martyrs). So we are not to regard suffering as the worst evil that can befall us. Sin is the worst evil that can befall us, and there is not always or necessarily a direct correlation between the sins we commit and the sufferings we experience.

RBS

SUBJECT: MINISTRY TO INDIVIDUALS VS. SOCIAL WITNESS

Dr. Steele,

I just had a quick question for you from Monday's class. We talked about working with individuals versus working to change the entire social order through organizations like the government. As I sat in class I was trying to think through Jesus' life to see if he ever tried to directly change the establishment. I could not think of any instances where he even attempted this in the manner we spoke of Monday. I think Jesus modeled an image of loving the world one person at a time. He stopped to talk with a Samaritan woman at the well; he took a boat across the Sea of Galilee only to free a demon-possessed man and then left; he forgave those who betrayed and killed him. I have never heard of any of the apostles staging protests and lobbying for new regulations. Please correct me if I am ignorant. But it seems we become just another one of the voices, like tobacco lobbyists, when this becomes our ministry. We are seen as a selfish grouping shouting and pushing for what we think is right. Maybe I am wrong, but it seems that the New Testament calls us to spend our time and energy loving individuals. How will making conditions better for people who are suffering (physically, economically) ever meet their deepest need? You cannot show somebody Christ and his love by merely fighting for rights away from those who are hurting. You have to be right next to people (sometimes this may need to turn into a protest), showing them God's love.

Thanks,

Joseph

Dear Joseph:

You make a strong case in favor of focusing one's ministry on individuals rather than the social order at large, and you have certainly drawn attention to a very serious danger of the latter approach, namely that the church can become strident in its tone and, far worse, can allow society rather than Christ to set the agenda for ministry. I have no argument with any of that.

However, I think the situation—both with respect to the kinds of ministry authorized by Scripture and with respect to the responsibilities Christians have in the world—is much more complex than your account might suggest. It is undeniably true that Jesus' ministry was often directed to "individuals." But his parables and his exorcisms must certainly be seen as part of his overall attempt to inaugurate the kingdom of God in a world that had fallen into the hands of evil powers—what

Paul will later call the "powers and principalities." And the ultimate consummation of that kingdom certainly entails a radical transformation of the social order. Moreover, his institution of a closely-knit community of disciples, with an inner circle of disciples the number of which was symbolic of the twelve tribes of Israel, was clearly intended as a challenge to the absolutistic pretensions of Rome and the collaborationism of the Sadducees and Herodians. This new community, which was supposed to lead a nonviolently revolutionary way of life, was to be a prophetic anticipation of the coming Kingdom. Furthermore, Jesus himself did, on at least one occasion, directly assault the worldly powers: in his driving of the moneychangers out of the temple. In this act, he placed himself squarely in the tradition of the Hebrew prophets, who routinely challenged the political and religious establishment of the Israelite state.

Furthermore, for Christians to refuse to challenge the evils of the social order on the grounds that authentic ministry must only be the care and evangelization of individuals, usually winds up meaning that the church becomes a silent collaborator with the status quo. At least that seems to me the unavoidable conclusion that we must draw when comparing and contrasting Frederick Douglass and Peter Cartwright on the question of the church's stance on slavery.[1]

RBS

NOTES

1 In my course on American Christianity, we read the autobiographies of Peter Cartwright, a frontier Methodist preacher, and Frederick Douglass, a runaway slave who became a senior American statesman.

CHAPTER 9

GENDER AND SEXUALITY ON A CHRISTIAN CAMPUS

There is an old joke that surfaces occasionally on my campus: if you're going to have sex in your dorm room, don't do it standing up, because if you're caught, you'll be expelled for dancing. Both the policy against dancing (which has since been repealed) and the joke (which has been around for a while) are revealing. The former reflects the ethic of sexual purity that prevails in evangelical communities like ours. The latter reflects the wide and widely known discrepancy between our ethical ideals and our actual behavior. Let's look at the ethic itself, and then at ways to deal with the awkward discrepancy between what we believe (or think we *should* believe) and the pressures we feel to live otherwise.

Put simply, the purity ethic is the "traditional" or "biblical" view on sexual conduct, or at least what most evangelicals regard as the traditional or biblical view. The body and its appetites are viewed with suspicion, and too much indulgence in physical pleasure and worldly luxury is deemed shameful. Sexual activity is restricted to the marriage bed. Pre-marital and extra-marital sex, masturbation, heavy petting, pornography, and homosexuality are taboo. Rules and safety procedures are needed to enforce these taboos. At a Christian college, this means dormitory curfews, chaperones and good lighting at social events, prohibitions against drinking and dancing, and (more recently) spam blockers and Internet filters. The assumption is that *purity* is the same as *innocence*, and that innocence is best preserved by preventing too much adolescent play and experimentation. Closely connected to this ethic of purity is a certain ideology of gender, according to which the social roles of men and women are strictly defined and sharply differentiated. The man is the "head" of the family: he is the breadwinner and has the final say on important decisions. The woman is the companion, the helpmeet, the chief cook and nurse for the whole family. A similar role differentiation is observed in many evangelical churches: men are the pastors, elders, deacons, and trustees; women are the Sunday school teachers, communion stewards, and coffee hour hostesses.

American culture in general no longer adheres to the ethic of purity or the ideology of gender just described—and this puts evangelicals in a bind. Should they try to maintain the old standards out of fidelity to the Bible, which, they believe, underwrites them? Or should they capitulate to the changes that have taken place in the surrounding culture at the risk of seeming irrelevant and antiquated? Let me give two illustrations of this dilemma.

A young man "confesses" to me that he is addicted to pornography and masturbates every night while viewing it. He's ridden with guilt. Prayer hasn't helped. Do I read him the riot act? That won't help, because his problem is not that he doesn't *respect* the moral standards, but that he can't live up to them. Adding fear to his guilt won't bring him emotional integrity or spiritual peace. Or do I tell him that he's making a mountain out of a molehill and that his "sin" is just a healthy libido? That won't help either, because it subverts the moral and spiritual standards on which his whole life is based and which, in the main, serve him quite well.

A young woman confides to me that she feels called to ordained ministry and wants to major in theology. I'm all set to congratulate her, but there are tears in her eyes. It turns out that her pastor and parents are scandalized by what she regards as a vocation from God. "Women can't be ministers," they tell her. "The Bible prohibits them from having spiritual authority over men!" Do I pat her on the head and suggest that she find a nice seminarian to marry and spend her life helping out in the nursery and running bake sales? That would trivialize her gifts and graces, and deny God's call on her life. Or do I rail at the asininity of her church's ordination policy? That would dishonor the very institution she wants to serve.

"Traditional" views of gender and sexuality should be subjected to serious theological and ethical critique. Such a critique ought to honor the moral authority of Scripture and the wisdom of the church's traditional norms, which the purity ethic professes to uphold. But it should also recognize that this wisdom has sometimes been accompanied by rather neurotic attitudes toward the human body and its functions and by harshly repressive strategies for keeping women "in their place."

As you learn about your body, desires, dreams and relationships, compare that to what church and society have told you. The church has established norms of sexual conduct, not because it regards the giving and receiving of sexual pleasure as an evil thing, but because it knows how easily such a *good* thing can be trivialized and exploited. Yet those who deviate from the norms—as we *all* do—are still within the reach of divine grace. We need to interpret what the Bible and the church say about gender roles through the lens of contemporary natural and social science, without romanticizing the social arrangements of first century Greco-Roman society—or nineteenth century American society. "Sexual purity" isn't a matter of avoiding forbidden pleasures, but of keeping sacred covenants. Obedience to God isn't a matter of fulfilling socially prescribed roles, but of carrying out the work God has gifted and called us to do.

SUBJECT: WOMEN IN THE CHURCH

Dr. Steele,

I have a question that doesn't really have to do with our discussions in class, but I feel that you might be able to give me your views on. The other day my friend Jesse and I were having a conversation regarding something my pastor preaches about, and Jesse felt it was heresy. Of course this alarmed and concerned me. I feel that Jesse is adequately equipped to say such a comment because of the fact that he is a Biblical Literature major over at

Northwest Bible College. Anyway, my pastor, more than once, has made it very clear that women are not to be deacons or pastors, that their role is for the teaching of women and children, but not of the congregation as a whole. Now I know that your wife is a minister, and I know a few women that are seeking to attend seminary. Jesse says that the translation of the Scriptures into English doesn't account correctly for this matter, and for my own personal interest, and in the interest of seeking out the truth, as always, I was looking to your opinion. Also, I feel like I was a little defensive when Jesse said that my pastor was preaching heresy, and if there is truth in his statement, I feel I owe him an apology.

I look forward to your response. Thank you, Dr. Steele. Enjoy your day.

Tessa

Hi Tessa!

Thanks for writing on this very important issue of women's leadership roles in the church. This is, indeed, a very hot topic in contemporary American church life, because, as Christians, we feel obliged to honor the moral authority of Scripture, but as Americans, we are naturally prone to egalitarianism. And since the Scriptures really do appear to endorse patriarchy (i.e., the dominance of men over women), we feel that if we opt for egalitarianism we are being unfaithful to Scripture, whereas we feel that if we opt to be faithful to Scripture we are endorsing an outdated and oppressive attitude toward women's social roles. I think several things need to be said here, partly in response to the issue as you and Jesse and your pastor have framed it, and partly with regard to the issue itself.

1. For one thing, the term "heresy" is always a polar coordinate with the term "orthodoxy." And "orthodoxy" is always understood as the set of doctrinal norms established by and governing the preaching of a *church* body. Preferably this would be the whole Body of Christ. (Thus the Apostles' Creed is a standard of orthodoxy that almost all Christians can subscribe to in some sense.) But in practice it is often smaller bodies, such as denominations or even congregations, which establish doctrinal norms. However, individuals should not be in the business of accusing other individuals of heresy, except insofar as they are the duly appointed and credentialed defenders of some church's doctrinal standards. Thus, I think your friend Jesse, while he may be accurately voicing the doctrinal standards of *his* church, is probably not in the position of making such accusations against the leader of *another* church, namely yours. There are, of course, serious disagreements among churches as to this issue—and many others. But then we have a problem of competing orthodoxies among different churches. And who is to say whose standard will be the rule by which all other doctrinal positions are to be judged?

2. That said, I think it is incontestable that the New Testament contains a number of passages that appear to reinforce the patriarchal social arrangements of ancient Jewish and Greco-Roman society. In those days, women were indeed denied many of the rights enjoyed by men, such as the right to own property, the right to give testimony in a court of law, and the right to govern. Many early Christian congregations appear

to have followed the prevailing cultural practices on this. Here, I think, your pastor is correct. And as far as I know, the patriarchal attitudes are reflected in the original Greek, and can't really be "translated away" without doing violence to the text.

3. On the other hand, not all early Christian churches took this route. There are many cases of women rising to positions of considerable influence in local Christian congregations. Read the closings of many of Paul's letters, and you will be amazed at the number of prominent women he names: Lydia, Prisca, Phoebe, Julia, Nympha, etc. Moreover, we have passages which appear to endorse something like a Christologically warranted egalitarianism—not identical, to be sure, to American democratic egalitarianism, but perhaps closer to that than the sort of patriarchy which wants to silence women or prevent them from taking leadership positions. Galations 3:26–28 explicitly denies that humanly imposed barriers of ethnicity and gender apply among the children of God, and Acts 2:17–21 explicitly states that the Holy Spirit will be poured out on men and women alike, and thus accords the privilege of public prophetic utterance to persons of both sexes. Here, I think, Jesse is quite right. And my hunch, although I don't know this for sure, is that his opinion has been shaped by the dominant theology of Northwest College. Northwest is sponsored by the Assemblies of God. AGs are Pentecostals, and Pentecostals base their gender egalitarianism on their doctrine of the Holy Spirit, which, in turn, is heavily influenced by their reading of the Acts of the Apostles.

4. And for what it is worth, here is my position: Although I am not a Pentecostal, I agree with the Pentecostal principle that the Spirit is free to summon whomever it wishes, male or

> female, to ordained ministry and positions of administrative leadership. But I do not think that inflammatory tactics like accusing those who disagree with this position of being "heretics" really helps very much, either to raise the status and role of women in the church or to bring the Body of Christ into ever closer conformity to the will of the Father.
>
> RBS

The following three email exchanges stemmed from a single session in my freshman "Christian Formation" class. That day we were studying a description of the seven deadly sins from *The Dark Night of the Soul* by St. John of the Cross.[1] When we got to lust, the conversation became very candid and self-revealing. I removed my jacket and tie, closed the textbook on the podium, and told the class that for the rest of the session I would be speaking not as their professor but as an older brother in Christ, who struggles with sexuality as much as they do.

SUBJECT: MASTURBATION

Dr. Steele,

I'm still speechless. I mean, I didn't know a class session could go like that. I mean that in a good way. Thank you for being honest with us about the "gray areas" that there aren't clear answers to. It really helps to know that sometimes, we (the students) aren't the only ones without certain answers.

I do have a question though. What is the bottom line on the masturbation issue? We basically came to the conclusion that there is no clear answer. I realize that more points were made against it than for it, however. I also noticed that you didn't bring up the opposing question, "Well, what do we do with our desires?" For non-sexually active males, that comes out as nocturnal emissions. Well, that's just fine usually, but in a dorm environment, that can be rather embarrassing, if you get my drift.

And masturbation—or simply sexual thoughts: Are the thoughts involved "lust" or "desire"?[2] I mean, I'll give a beet-red example: I've been with my girlfriend for sixteen months on Monday. She's my first kiss and my first love. We plan to get married. If I find myself thinking sexual thoughts about her, is that "lust" or is it "desire"? We aren't going to have sex before we get married. We're firm on that. I'm not saying that we don't make out, but doesn't "making out" in *my* situation (after well over a year) have a little different meaning than my making out with a girl I just met four days ago? I would really like to think of it as an expression of my love for her. I really try to be sensitive to her needs. It's *really* easy to see that guys and girls are built completely differently when it comes to emotion/sexuality. I try to be there for her in every way, especially emotionally. And I try my very hardest not to ever objectify her for my pleasure. Well, there's a lot of rambling. My question is simply this: am I lusting or desiring when I think about her?

I hope it's okay that I share this with you. This class period today just really brought up a lot of issues that, as you said, make life as an eighteen-year-old Christian with a conscience very awkward indeed.

Sincerely,

Stephen

Stephen,

My apologies for failing to reply to your post until this afternoon, and my thanks for prodding me about this earlier today. Here goes, for what it's worth:

1. On masturbation: The Bible gives us almost no help here. The one reference, and it is so exceedingly oblique as to be virtually irrelevant, is Genesis 38, where Onan is condemned for "spilling his seed" on the ground, rather than impregnating his deceased brother's widow and thus "raising up children for his brother." There are no explicit prohibitions elsewhere, unless one assumes (as, admittedly, Christians have generally tended to assume) that masturbation falls under the very general prohibitions of "fornication." It is certainly true that some things that are often associated with masturbation, such as pornography, can be morally condemned on the grounds that they exploit and objectify human beings, and it is also true that in some

cases masturbation (and/or viewing pornography) can be a form of psychological rejection against those with whom we ought to be sexually and emotionally intimate, namely our spouses. But I simply can't see how these cases translate into an absolute and unqualified condemnation of the practice. This is not to say that I am *approving* of the practice, or *recommending* it. I just mean that I find the moral disapproval that is often registered against it hard to understand, and the terrible shame that many men and women feel about engaging in the practice regrettable. What that says about dormitory conduct, I just don't know. But the toilet stalls have latches for a reason.

2. Judging from what you have said about your relationship with your girlfriend, I would say you have both a very healthy and a very holy thing going with her, for which I rejoice and thank God! The decision to delay intercourse until marriage is *very, very* wise, and as long as both of you observe prudent boundaries when you "make out" (e.g., keeping your clothes on) and do nothing that makes either of you uncomfortable or forces either of you to do something shameful, painful, humiliating, or dangerous, it would seem to me that you are conducting yourselves responsibly and maturely.

Best,

RBS

SUBJECT: PREMARITAL SEX

Dr. Steele,

That was deep! But I was wondering why you didn't take a more absolute stand on premarital sex? I'm not saying that you should have, but I am wondering if you didn't because you just didn't want to pounce on Tony's opinion and maybe stop the flow of discussion? Of course I understand the logic of that argument.[3] Many of the world's ways of doing things have logic, but that doesn't make it permissible. I think Bill's comment on the trying-out-the-coat analogy was wonderful, and I hope it got those boys thinking.[4] The whole conversation was very insightful. Especially when you gave your definition of lust. I always did think of lust as just that desire, but never thought of it as creating an object of someone and treating them like an "it." It makes me think more that some of those feelings we experience *are* simply our endocrine systems, and natural desires that are created in every human. For me, I think it would become the sin, when I allow those thoughts to dwell and linger in my head. Like you said, it's nice to just put those thoughts aside slowly and re-focus your attention on what's important. Thanks for being so open and honest with us again.

Sonya

P.S. I am glad that those comments were made on premarital sex because I think it opens our eyes to other views people have and allows us to deal with those, and

ask ourselves, or challenge ourselves to why we believe in
what we do.

Dear Sonya:

Yes, it *was* deep! I'm still a bit stunned from the extraordinary
candor shown by so many students on so many delicate
subjects. To answer your first question, you are quite right
that my main reasons (pedagogically) for not "pouncing on
Tony's opinion" were (1) not wanting to silence discussion
and (2) not wanting to humiliate him (or anyone else) by flatly
calling him "wrong" or "immoral" or what have you. But I had
other, more "personal" reasons, too, including the fear of
being hypocritically moralistic in making pronouncements on
issues in which my own past conduct was hardly exemplary—
even though, as I reflect on that often disgraceful conduct
twenty-five years later, now that I am married, and ordained,
and a moral theologian, I can unhesitatingly take a "more
absolute stand" against premarital sex. That is, it's easy for
a happily married middle-aged man to pontificate against
the "sins of youth" (cf. Ps. 25:7), but such pontification does
not really do much good for young people who are dealing
with raging hormones and intense physical desires for which
there seem to be no "holy" means of gratification. The moral
issues are not resolved by flat, official prohibitions. But at the
same time I certainly don't think that the mere fact that sexual
desires are so terribly difficult to control implies that anything
goes. The moral issues are complex and delicate, and I was
trying to indicate that by my somewhat equivocal manner of
responding to student questions and comments. Yet what
was problematic for me is that I certainly don't want my
"equivocal manner" in class to be construed as tantamount

to "permissiveness." I was stuck, and I only hope that people benefited from the honest exchange itself, even if they didn't come away with any easy answers.

RBS

SUBJECT: LUST

Dear Professor Steele,

I thought it was great to talk about all that we talked about in class. I think a lot of times we young guys get down on ourselves for our lusts. We do need to confront these sins and work to stop them, but God understands our struggles, and sometimes I think we can be better off having remorse for these sins and still be able to keep our heads up (a little) so as not to let these sins totally bring us off our walk. I don't know if this makes sense, but that's a little bit about what I have experienced. Maybe my thoughts are wrong though and I misunderstood your point.

Ben

Dear Ben,

Thanks for your affirmation of the way I handled Friday's class session. It was a delicate subject, and I was frankly amazed at the level of self-disclosure displayed by the class. But I do think that candor in these matters is better than avoidance, because sex presses itself on us whether we like it or not. And if Christian pastors and professors and parents are going to help our young people have a healthy sexual ethic we have to say more about it than just, "Don't do it, and don't even think about it, and when you do it and/or think about it, feel guilty." That approach is just not helpful, especially in a culture where all the messages in the media are exactly the opposite. TV, film, and the internet all tell us, "Think about it all the time, get as much of it as you can, and don't let 'morality' get in your way." Moralism and secrecy breed confusion and a certain amount of hypocrisy, but the modern commercialism of sex breeds absolute personal and social chaos. So what is the alternative?

As near as I can figure—and I've thought a lot about this, but still have lots of questions and uncertainties—Christians need to see the issue something like this: (1) Sex is not "wrong" or "dirty" as such. It is a feature of our created nature, the expression of which is, under the proper circumstances, healthy and beautiful and godly. (2) But sex is a powerful force within us, and therefore potentially dangerous to ourselves and others, and when its expression is not protected by the marital covenant, people get hurt. Sexual "experimentation" leads very quickly into sexual exploitation, even when it is mutually consensual. And although the marital covenant does not guarantee that there will be no exploitation by either partner of the other, the lack of any formal commitment such as the marriage vows makes exploitation and objectification perilously easy. (3) Sex cannot be completely shut out of our consciousness by sheer will power, and although guilt for thinking about it can, to a certain extent, suppress sexual thoughts, it can't eliminate them entirely and only makes them go "underground," where we can't see them or work with them. (4) Nor can sex be completely shut out of our consciousness by even the most ardent religious faith. Indeed, as John of the Cross tells us, prayer itself can actually trigger sexual thoughts and desires, because of "the physical pleasure which the body takes in spiritual things."[5] Thus spirituality and sexuality are connected at a very deep level in us, and while as Christians we believe that our faith can and should be a moral guide and a moral force for controlling our sexual conduct, we should not think of that in a superstitious way, as if saying the "right" prayers or saying prayers with enough fervor could magically make sexual thoughts go away. Such an idea simply makes people feel guilty when it turns out not to work that way. At the same time, the deployment of spiritual resources can indeed help us to come to terms with the waywardness of our fantasies and desires, alert us to the dangers of expressing these by promiscuous and addictive behavior, and help us to place them before God for healing and maturation. That is, it can rescue us from the despair and sense of futility that arises in us when we realize that our bodies tend to "zig" where our Christian values "zag." God is indeed with us in the struggles, understanding our plight and offering us mercy and strength.

RBS

SUBJECT: LATE BLOOMER[6]

Dr. Steele,

I've been thinking again (not too seriously, though), and I was hoping you might have some wisdom to impart to me. So, I'm a 23-year-old woman living in a house with six men. It's probably enough just to say that, but I'll elaborate. During college I had a lot of male friends, and I always sort of prided myself on being "one of the guys." Late bloomer that I am, I have realized in the past few months that I am *not* a guy. Along with that has come the realization that I find my male friends attractive and they find me attractive, too. Before I had these realizations, sexuality and committed love were inseparable in my mind. But now things have changed. All of a sudden I am perceptive to sexual tension/energy between myself and quite a few other people. (I hope it's okay to talk to you about such a personal issue. But you even said yourself that you are nosy by nature, so this time I just won't wait for you to pry it out of me. Besides, I think it's a shame that sexuality isn't discussed more often, especially within the church.) I am realizing that I am a sexual being, that I don't feel guilty about it, and that I don't find the standard Christian imperatives to "save yourself until marriage" very compelling at all. It has really become an issue now that I am not taking myself and my actions so seriously. I'm not about to eliminate all boundaries entirely, but I am interested in charting out that middle ground between unhealthy suppression and no boundaries because that's where most of us actually live out our lives.

I'd love to hear your thoughts on this issue if you are inclined to share them.

Rose

Okay, first off, who are you and what have you done with my friend Rose?

Just kidding. Actually, it's very wonderful to see you facing this set of questions so squarely and maturely. Let me say a few very general things for starters:

- Yes, it's true that you are *not* a guy. Congratulations!

- Yes, it's true that you *are* a sexual being. Congratulations again!

- Yes, it's true that I'm nosy by nature, and I assure you that I am very happy to talk about this subject (or any other subject) with you. Thanks for writing.

- Yes, it's true, sexuality isn't discussed much in the church. And it's not *discussed* much in secular society either, although it is endlessly joked about and capitalized on. In my opinion, the commercialization and sensationalization of sexuality in secular society are quite as bad as, and perhaps worse than, its repression in the church. Moreover, the people in secular society who do talk seriously about sexuality do not always address its moral and spiritual dimensions. They tend to emphasize its biological and psychological dimensions.

- I wholeheartedly endorse your effort to find "middle ground between unhealthy suppression and no boundaries," and I agree that that is "where most of us actually live out our lives." The way I would put it is this:

- Sex is a wonderful thing, something to be celebrated and enjoyed.

- But sex is also dangerous thing, something to be handled with caution. Hence the need for "boundaries."

- There is no such thing as "casual sex," except among lamentably trivial people. If being human is morally serious business, and if sexuality is a crucial part of being human, then sexuality is very serious business, too. The fact that sex is so delightful is precisely why it mustn't be casual. We can't afford to degrade or trifle with anything so central to our humanity.

- Neither is there any such thing as "safe sex," regardless of what kind of "precautions" one may use against unwanted pregnancy and sexually transmitted diseases. For people who are united psychologically and physically by intercourse are very likely to be injured if they are not also united morally and spiritually by covenant.

- Chastity is not the same as celibacy. One can have a chaste marriage and still be having a lot of great sex. One can also be formally celibate but terribly preoccupied by and hung up about sex.

- Neither is chastity the same as repression. One can have healthy attitudes about one's own body and its needs and desires without necessarily being sexually active. One can also be very sexually active without having healthy attitudes about one's body.

All of this is very general, of course. What it has to say about your relationships with the guys in your house or your own awakening sense of yourself as a sexual person is unclear. Perhaps the time has come for another of our little "chats."

Warm regards,

RBS

SUBJECT: HOMOSEXUALITY

Professor Steele,

I was reflecting on our discussion in class today and was reminded of a religion class I took my senior year in high school. In this class we examined social issues and the perspectives the main worldviews had relating to these issues. During our section on homosexuality we encountered an interesting take on our being created in the "image of God." I wanted to tell it to you and have a response to it.

We watched a video debate between a man who claimed homosexuality is acceptable in the eyes of God and a man who claimed it was immoral. The man who claimed it was immoral used the following as a contention for his position: In Genesis we see the creation of man, and God says "Let us make man in our own image." In the Hebrew language the word for all of mankind is used in reference to Adam, and it is only after Eve is created that we see the word for man in the sense of gender and we also see the word for female. He argued that when man and woman are joined together they are completing the image of God in mankind. In other words, mankind was created in God's image and both male and female possess different aspects of the image of God. They also both possess some of the same attributes of God's image. So he argued homosexuality is wrong because woman and woman or man and man cannot complete the image of God, which he argued was one of the primary purposes of marriage along with procreation (neither of which could be done in a homosexual relationship).

I guess my main questions would be (1) Is there really a distinction in the Hebrew text between Adam representing all of mankind before the loss of his rib, and Adam representing the male gender after the creation of Eve? (2) If so, does his inference (man and woman combined complete the image of God) from this fact work? (3) If it does, what does it do to those who choose a life of singleness? (4) In general your reaction to this idea.

I hope I explained this thoroughly and thank you for your time,

Camille

Dear Camille,

In my view, the person on the video has not given a very persuasive argument. There may well be good "natural law" arguments against homosexuality (i.e., that it violates our nature as "designed" by God), but I don't think his exegesis of Genesis works. The name "Adam" comes from the Hebrew word *adamah*, which means earth or soil. In other words, "Adam" means something like "Earthling"—not in contrast, say, to "Martian," but in the sense that human beings are nurtured from the produce of the earth, and after they die their bodies return to the earth. (Hence the phrase in the funeral liturgy, "Ashes to ashes, and dust to dust.") Needless to say, this is true of all persons, regardless of gender or sexual orientation. Thus, in the first of the two accounts in Genesis of the creation of humankind (Genesis 1:26–31), God says, "Let us make humankind [*adam*] in our image, according to our likeness" (v. 26), and a few lines later the author comments, "So God created humankind [*adam*] in his image, in the image of God he created them; male and female he created them" (v. 27)

In the second account of creation (Genesis 2:4b–25), "man" [*adam*] is created "from the dust of the ground" (v. 7). God soon realizes that it is not good for "man" to be alone, and then that the other creatures will not suffice him for companionship. So God creates woman, a move that "the man" finds delightful! He exclaims, "This at last is bone of my bones and flesh of my flesh; this one shall be called Woman [*ishshah*], for out of Man [*ish*] this one was taken" (v. 23). Here sexual differentiation is described frankly (although there is as yet no hint that the woman, the "helper" and "partner" of the man, is in any way inferior in rank to him or exists solely to serve and please him). This sexual differentiation and partnership relation is construed to be the basis of marriage (v. 24). And of course there isn't any doubt that sexual differentiation is biologically requisite for reproduction.

But to say that people need the companionship of others, and particularly of members of the "opposite sex" (funny expression!), in order to flourish is not to say that apart from marriage the image of God is somehow incomplete in any individual. Indeed, that flatly contradicts the earlier account, which explicitly says that members of both sexes are made in the image of God, not that members of each sex are made in one half of the image of God. Would one want to say that Jesus and Paul, neither of whom ever married, were somehow deficient in humanity? Surely not. (Actually, the argument of the person on the film is much closer to that of the pagan philosopher, Plato, than it is to the Bible. In Plato's *Symposium*, one of the characters, the comic poet Aristophanes, argues, tongue in cheek, that human beings were originally spherical in shape, and that when they grew so arrogant that they ignored the gods, the gods took revenge by cutting them down the middle. From that point forward each half would spend the remainder of his or her life wobbling around, looking for a mate to complete him or her.)

So on the basis of Genesis 1–3, I think it is possible to say this: (1) Human beings are meant to live in community with one another. (2) One of the most basic forms of human community, which God explicitly blesses, is marriage and family. (3) One of the ways that we honor the sanctity of our marriage vows and parental responsibilities is by remembering that our spouses are persons of infinite dignity and worth, being made, like ourselves, in God's image. But none of this implies that every single person is cut out for or called to marriage, or that those who never marry are somehow defective. I'm not sure what this implies when it comes to making a moral assessment of homosexuality. But I am sure that it *can't* mean that gay and lesbian persons are not made in God's image every bit as much as straight people are. There is no way the Genesis text can be made to say that.

Yours,

RBS

NOTES

1 Excerpted in Richard J. Foster and James Bryan Smith, *Devotional Classics: Selected Readings for Individuals and Groups* (San Francisco: HarperCollins Publishers, 1993), 33–39.

2 Stephen sets "desire" and "lust" in quotation marks because I had drawn a distinction between them that morning. I had suggested that sexual "desire" *per se* is not a moral evil, but a biological and psychological condition of possibility for human reproduction and marital stability, whereas "lust" is evil because it regards the other primarily as a instrument of self-gratification. The covenant of marriage—or at least the firm and stated intention by both partners to enter into that covenant—is our primary way of mapping the moral difference between them.

3 Tony was a student who openly rejected Christianity and ridiculed its moral teachings. He had espoused the view that there is nothing wrong with recreational sex.

4 I shared with the class a statement that one of my wife's parishioners had made to her in a premarital counseling session: "Of course we've had sex before marriage! You wouldn't buy a coat without trying it on, would you?" Bill had replied that the analogy was a good example of how recreational

sex, even with one's fiancée, entails the objectification of one's partner. Determining marital compatibility is not the same as making a purchase.

5 *Op. cit.*, 35.

6 The author of this post had taken several courses from me at SPU, and we had corresponded and spoken privately many times during and after her college years about various personal and intellectual matters. Thus, this email exchange differs from most of the others in this book in two ways: its author was not a student of mine at the time of writing and its contents have nothing directly to do with course material. Still, it seems appropriate to include here, since it gives a very illuminating sketch of the emotional maturation— and the accompanying moral puzzlements—that take place during and just after the college years.

CHAPTER 10

THE "PROBLEM" OF HUMAN SUFFERING

Theological questions are seldom purely "theoretical." At some level, they are usually "existential." They reflect the puzzlements and predicaments of life. This is particularly clear when we look at the questions people ask about human suffering.

If you were to ask me, "Why must people suffer?" I'd answer, "Which people?" You might regard that as a very callous remark, and suspect me of being partial or prejudiced, as if I thought that the suffering of some people—*my* family, *my* friends, or *myself*—was more worrisome than the suffering of others—strangers, foreigners, or enemies. You want to know why an all-powerful, all-loving God permits suffering *at all*—*to anyone*! Now, I won't deny that I'm sometimes guilty of partiality and prejudice. But that isn't what drives me to wonder whom, in particular, you mean when you ask why "people" in general must suffer.

It's because people in general *don't* suffer. Individuals suffer. Now, it's true that *all* individuals suffer at times. It's also true that individuals sometimes suffer because they belong to certain groups (e.g., oppressed minorities) or live in certain places (say, in the path of a hurricane), and are therefore victims of injustices or catastrophes that are shared by others. (And shared suffering undoubtedly has a quality quite different from private suffering.) Still, the locus of pain and sorrow—and therefore the proper object of compassion—is always the individual.

So, you ask me, "Why must people suffer?" What I start wondering is: "What drives *you* to ask *this* question at *this* time?" There are three obvious possibilities. First, you yourself (or someone close to you) might be suffering right now, and you are trying to come to terms with that. But out of courtesy, you cast what is really a very concrete, practical question *for you* into an abstract, hypothetical question *for me*. If that is the case, let me say how much I appreciate your unwillingness to burden me with your problem. That is a tribute to your tact and courage. But precisely for that reason, it has the effect of arousing my interest and compassion. And so my question, "Which people?" callous as it may sound, is quite the opposite: it is *my* attempt to invite *you* to disclose whatever you wish about your situation, so that I may enter into it more fully, so that I may be as "present" to you as you may wish me to be. The truth is, I have no idea why you or anyone else must suffer. But I am willing to hear the story of your suffering or the suffering of the one you love, not so that I can explain it to you, but so that I can help you find whatever human meaning and divine consolation it may bear for you.

Second, it might not be you or yours whose suffering is on your mind just now. It might be the suffering of someone at a distance to you. The general question, "Why must people suffer?" often gets asked in the wake of horrendous catastrophes—the 9/11 attacks, the Indian Ocean tsunami, Hurricane Katrina, and so forth. You are wondering what responsibility you have to the victims—who are, in one sense, far removed from you, but whose plight has been brought home to you by all the media attention. Again, it is a tribute to your moral sensitivity that you wonder about your duty. But you have phrased the question in a way that comes perilously close to exempting you from it. You have set me up to tell you "why" God permits such tragedies, and thus to collaborate with you in turning the victims into nameless, faceless "others," topics of academic conversation, and perhaps objects of polite, detached pity, but not persons to whom you (and I) must extend care. Once again, my callous-sounding answer, "Which people?" is intended to skunk out the story behind your question, and thus to keep us both where we belong: attentive to *who* is suffering, and *how*, and *what* we ought to be doing about it.

Let me put all this another way. The question, "Why must people suffer?" is a way of asking a profoundly theological question *un*-theologically.[1] For it assumes that God is involved in human suffering as its unexplained *cause*. The Bible doesn't deny this. But its central witness is that God comes to those who suffer as an *unseen companion* and *comforting presence*. On the scriptural account, the mystery of suffering is not *why* God permits it, but *what* God does about it—and beyond that, what God expects God's people to do about it. To the extent that my response to your question is faithful to scripture, it will help you see that although we can't know *why* (in theory) people suffer—or why *people* (in general) suffer—we can nevertheless experience the touch of God's grace in the midst of our own sufferings and be the instruments of that grace in the midst of the sufferings of our neighbors, near and far.

That's not to say that you and I shouldn't discuss the various "answers" to the problem of human suffering—that it's a test of faith, or a consequence of finitude and creatureliness, or a punishment for sin, etc. Assessing the plausibility of these answers is a useful exercise. But its usefulness is due to the fact that it shows that the idea that suffering is a problem in itself deeply problematic. The answers to the why-question fail. But the fact that they fail doesn't falsify the gospel for those who have actually experienced God's presence in the midst of suffering, or have felt God's call to help those who suffer. It elucidates the fact that the Christian gospel is not a theoretical explanation of why things are as they are, but a witness to the One who meets us where we are. Divine salvation isn't an answer to our questions, but a response to our needs—healing for our pains, friendship in our loneliness, and consolation in our bereavement

It is something else, too: it is forgiveness for our sins. This brings us to the third reason you might be asking why people must suffer. You might be burdened with guilt over sin, and imagine that your own or someone else's suffering is a divine punishment for it. Where sin is involved, what may look like an expression of compassionate concern may be nothing more than a mask for prurient curiosity. So I won't ask you to tell me too much. But I will certainly probe your assumption that human sin somehow "explains" human suffering, that it inevitably brings divine retribution. How will I do this?

I'll refer to the Bible, of course. Now, admittedly the scriptural evidence on this issue is equivocal. There *are* biblical texts that treat suffering as a "natural" consequence of sin, or even as a direct divine punishment for it (e.g., Genesis 3:14–19; Romans 6:23a). These assert that God has arranged the universe so that our sins and follies ultimately recoil upon our own heads. But a second group of biblical texts loosen or sever the relation between sin and suffering. They don't deny that God governs human events wisely and justly, but they do deny that human beings can ever fathom God's purposes and timing. Hence they reject the notion that the severity of a person's sins can be deduced from the intensity of her sufferings, and thus prohibit us from regarding the victims of *mis*-fortune as grossly *un*-righteous and unworthy of our care. Preeminent among this second group of texts are certain sayings of Jesus, who regarded sufferers as the objects, not of God's wrath, but of God's redemptive compassion, and who regarded indifference to the sufferings of others as the very quintessence of sin (Luke 13:1–5; John 9:1–3).

The most extensive biblical treatment of the question of the relation between sin and suffering is the Book of Job. Job, a righteous and hitherto prosperous man, is suddenly overwhelmed with calamities, which, he insists, are undeserved and therefore, on the traditional view, inexplicable. He is attended in his sufferings by several friends, who, after a respectful period of silence, try to persuade him that in a morally ordered universe, one's sufferings are exactly proportional to one's sins. The debate is settled in Job's favor when God himself enters the fray and rebukes Job's friends for defending divine justice all too cleverly—and therefore wrongly (Job 42:7–9). But God's own repudiation of the principle that human sufferings are the consequence of divine judgments implies that divine justice, which *does* indeed rule the universe, is finally incomprehensible to human beings. When God addresses Job "out of the whirlwind" (38:1), it is not to answer Job's question of why he had been subjected to so many trials and tribulations. On the contrary, God "answers" Job with a series of crushing questions of his own: "Who is this . . . ? Where were you . . . ? Do you know . . . ?" So although God vindicates Job for *asking* the why-question, God himself does not *answer* it. Furthermore, God censures the comforters for supposing that *they* have the theologically correct answer. Thus, God honors the sufferer's demand for an explanation of his misfortune, not by satisfying that demand as such, but by displaying love and respect for the sufferer himself. Moreover, God decrees that those who would render comfort to the sufferer must *share* his sorrows, not *explain* them. Hence, the book of Job affirms that the human tendency to regard suffering as a direct consequence of sin is both simple-minded and hard-hearted. Suffering is an enigma that defies intellectual penetration and brings our academic theorizing to a halt. But it evokes a response from God—and demands a response from us.

You may be unhappy to learn that the Bible casts doubt on the notion that sin and suffering are related as cause to effect. You may prefer to think that God's moral order is designed along such "rational" lines, and presume that theology can explain—and thereby justify—the way things are. I disagree, and I will challenge you to work out the moral consequences of your position from the perspective of the sufferer, not the perspective of the judge.

I return to my key point: The problem of suffering vividly indicates something about *all* theological inquiry, namely, that it is personal, existential, and practical. This doesn't mean that we must speak autobiographically whenever we theologize. But it does mean that real-life issues may underlie what look like purely academic questions.

SUBJECT: "WHY DID GOD LET MY BABY DIE?"

Dear Dr. Steele:

I have been pondering this thought for a couple days now. You told us the story of the lady who was having a really hard time giving up the fact that she lost her son. She asked you, "Why did God let my baby die?"[2] You said that the point of that was to make us feel her pain when we hear her say that. My question is: Isn't there *anything* we can say to help people understand and bear their sufferings? I know there isn't really any pat answer. We don't have the capability of understanding God when it comes to this kind of stuff, but do we just have to let it go? Do we have to say, in a way, there is nothing we can do and push it behind us? That is where I am a little confused. How *do* we deal with those questions and situations?

Thanks,

Alison

Dear Alison:

You ask what we can do when someone asks such a searing, searching question as, "Why did God let my baby die?" It may be good for *us* simply to feel the pain behind such a question, but that alone doesn't help the woman who is mourning the loss of her child. What do we say to *her?* Or do we, as you say, "just have to let it go, say there is nothing we can do, and push it behind us"? According to your letter, this is where you are "confused."

Believe me, this is where I'm confused, too! I've been pondering the question for over twenty years, and I'm not sure I have come to a satisfactory answer. I have come to believe one thing, however, and that is that we must *live* the question. We must let it nag at us, and not try to "let it go" or "push it behind us." That is, the very unanswerableness of the question does some important work in our souls: it makes us share in the pain and tragedy of the world, which people who are white and healthy and reasonably well-to-do (like me!) seldom experience directly.

Of course, all of us have struggles and troubles. But many of our struggles and troubles pale in comparison with the kinds of appalling disasters that occur daily in, say, urban American ghettos and rural Third World villages. Yet the problem is that we don't see them because we are insulated from them by our busy, comfortable, middle-class lives. However, every once in a while disasters *do* come close to home, maybe not to ourselves, but to people of our acquaintance. That was what happened when I went to visit that bereaved woman in upstate Vermont. Suddenly I was in the presence of a kind of misery that I had never witnessed before—though as a pastor I have witnessed it, and as a parent of a severely disabled child I have experienced it personally, many times since.

And the unanswerableness of the question, "Why do such terrible things as the deaths of innocent children happen in God's good world?" has had a marvelously sobering effect on me. It has made me more sensitive to other people than I am naturally prone to be, more patient in the presence of suffering, less anxious to run away and bury myself in my own activities and projects.

Okay, fine. That's what the unanswerableness of the "Why?" question has done for *me*. But what about the people who *ask* the question? What can I say to *them*? To be truthful, I'm simply not sure. But I'm also not sure that what they really need is a ready-made answer from me. I think what they really need from me is to have me not run away from them simply because I have no answer to their question. That is, what they need from me is my faithful presence, my undivided attention, my patient concern for their anguish, my compassion. I may not be able to explain why evil has befallen them, but I can at least offer them a cup of tea, a shoulder to cry on, and a genuine interest in looking at their scrapbooks and photo albums of the deceased.

In themselves, such things may seem very insignificant. But what they communicate, perhaps at a subliminal level, is this: "I am with you, and the Holy One whom I serve is with you, in this time of sorrow. I cannot 'answer your questions' or 'take away your sorrow.' But I can assure you by my very willingness to stay with you in the midst of your questions and sorrow that you are precious in God's eyes, and that God will, in his own way and in his own time, transform your questions into faith and sanctify your sorrow with his grace."

Yours,

RBS

SUBJECT: MINISTERING TO A SUFFERING YOUTH

Hello Dr. Steele,

Right now I'm in two classes—yours and another—that have talked about evil, both natural and moral, and how it causes suffering, pain, etc. I can understand natural disasters, and even evil caused by one human hurting another. Well, I don't understand why one does this, but I do think I have a fairly good idea of free will and how that gift allows people to do things and consequences have to be suffered, even by the victim and how God can help us through those times, but He is not the direct cause of them. But my questions then come on the subject of people with disabilities. I appreciated what you said in class, how you don't believe God punished you or your wife or Sarah by inflicting her with her disease, and how it has made you ask different kinds of questions regarding your role in loving her, being a father, loving God. I am getting my endorsement in Special Education, and I am a leader for Young Life Open Door,[3] so this topic hits fairly close to home for me.

At club there are kids with various disabilities, and I know life is difficult for each of them and their life has been much harder than mine has. These kids are amazing! In working with and spending time with them I know that many of them experience God's love and don't hold God responsible for their disability. One girl I was talking to, however, doesn't have a physical disability, but some sort of mental disability. I'm not sure exactly what it is. She is very bright; she can be very fun, but I know that she suffers an extreme amount, to the point of wanting to seriously hurt herself. From talking to her it seems that her school is not a great environment, and she is taunted by schoolmates. It is difficult for me to understand this sort of impairment and how God plays a role. I realize God loves this girl and cares for her, and is hurt when she is hurt. When I was talking to her the other day though about her difficulties she said she knew she should believe in God and love Him, but sometimes it is hard because one part of her wants to hurt herself. As I was telling her that God does truly care for her I found myself asking what I would think if our places were reversed. How could I believe that a loving God permits this disease to be in me that wants me to inflict pain on myself? That makes me the target of jokes and teasing and pranks? I don't know if I would believe someone telling me this if I were her. How can I tell her that God created her with love, and does love her, yet she has this disability that has put her in the hospital for suicidal attempts?

Surely God does not want his people to suffer so. To me this doesn't seem to correlate with a natural or moral evil, it seems totally opposite of God. I'm sure there isn't an easy answer to this, perhaps this is one of those subjects I'll never know the answer to. But I would like to hear what you have to say or talk about it with you.

Thank you,

Holly

Dear Holly,

Your post is extremely moving to me, and I would treasure the opportunity to talk with you personally about it. For there are at least two issues—distinct, though obviously related—that have to be disentangled here. First, what does your friend need to hear to help her bear her particular cross? And second, how do you think about and respond to your friend's situation in a theologically astute and spiritually balanced manner. Disentangling these two things (and perhaps some other issues that are less obvious to us at the moment) will take some time, and probably ought to be done face-to-face, rather than by email. So let's get together some time soon. I'll try to remember to bring my calendar to class tomorrow, and we can, if you like, set an appointment.

In the meantime, and for what it's worth, let me "paste" here a paragraph from a post I sent to another student of mine who recently asked for my advice on what she described as her "habit of self-destructive behavior." She didn't want to talk about it face to face, or to elaborate on the details, and only wanted "generic advice" on the situation. This is what I wrote:

> Well, the most pertinent generic advice I would give to someone who reports habits of self-destructive behavior would be what Martin Luther used to tell himself when he was assaulted by melancholia and despair: "Remember, Martin, you are baptized." If one thinks long and hard about what God says to a person when that person receives baptism, one should find a great deal of comfort and strength: "You," says God, "are mine. You are mine because I love you. I love you in spite of all the reasons you have to believe yourself unlovely and unlovable. I have named you and claimed you in this ceremony because I have high hopes and great plans for you.

> Please don't hurt yourself, because that would suggest
> that my promises to you are invalid or insignificant or
> ineffective. I won't coerce you into being kind to yourself,
> but I will go to any ends necessary, including Good
> Friday, to invite you to belong to the Easter People."

I'm not at all sure that this kind of thing would be helpful to your friend. My friend said these words helped her very much, but she is considerably older and has a deep Christian faith. Your friend, on the other hand, is presumably a teenager and seems to have doubts as to whether to believe in God at all. So maybe my words to my friend won't work well for yours, though you are certainly welcome to try them on her, or adapt them to her case, or simply pass them on to her for what they may be worth.

I do think, however, that two key issues that you will have to address with your friend at some point are buried in her statement that "she knows she should believe in God and love Him, but sometimes it is hard because one part of her wants to hurt herself." First, if she thinks of believing as something she "should" do, she may be experiencing guilt for not doing it, and that guilt itself may contribute to her desire to hurt herself. Faith is not a duty that we are supposed to perform; it is a free response of love and gratitude for a gift already given, namely the gift of God's love. Thus the accent of pastoral care should not fall on her *failure* to do something she should (i.e., conjure up something called "belief"), but rather on the *good news* that she is already loved, just as she is, disability and all. Second, she is not likely to come to the kind of joyous faith that may help her *handle* her disability *if* she thinks that God is somehow responsible for her disability or owes her a cure for it *before* she believes in him. Faith is not bargaining, but trust. It does not say: "If you do so-and-so for me [heal me of my disability], I will do such-and-such for you [believe in you]." Rather, it says: "Because you have already shown your great love for me in Christ, I can rely on you to help me through my struggles with self-destructive impulses, unpopularity at school, etc."

But let us talk further about these difficult, delicate, and troubling matters.

RBS

SUBJECT: QUESTIONS ABOUT HEALING

Dear Dr. Steele,

I've always had questions about healing, and I have a certain ailment right now that is not comfortable at all and I'm wondering if Christians are just missing out on some promise that God gave us that we could be healed when we needed it. I know at least in my life, healing was never talked about much at church or school and was just referred to when talking about miracles that Jesus or the disciples did in the Bible. I have heard many stories of people being healed in this day and age though, which really makes me wonder. At my church, they follow the procedure of healing in the Bible found in James 5:14–15. The elders of the church come and anoint the person's head with oil and lay hands on them and pray for them to be healed. Some are healed and some aren't. Then there is the type of healing I see on TV, where just a prayer and a touch by a certain person can heal a person instantly. A friend and I were looking at the verses in James and we were wondering what the words "sick" and "well" and all the other words in those verses were translated from in the Greek, and were wondering if something could have been lost or gained in the translation. I just don't see the point in suffering through what I'm going through if there's a way for it to be healed. I know God can do anything—that is obvious to me, and I don't totally understand why there would need to be a formula for being healed, but then again, it is simply impossible for me to ever understand the ways of God. As you can tell, I'm sure, I am confused. Thank you for taking the time to read this. It really does mean a lot to me.

Sincerely,

Matt

Dear Matt,

Thank you for your post regarding healing. I hope I can shed a bit of light on your questions. First, the biblical words for "disease" and "health" bear pretty much the same meaning as the contemporary English words. True, the ancients thought somewhat differently about the causes and cures of many diseases than we do, and were more inclined than we are to regard illnesses and disabilities as signs of divine wrath or as the consequence of demonic visitation. So, too, they tended to regard healers and miracle-workers with considerable

religious veneration and awe—although modern people
sometimes regard doctors in a very similar way. So in that
sense there was a more direct connection between "religion"
and "health" than we tend to make today in our health care
system, dominated as it is by science and technology. But
matters of biblical translation do not, I think, really affect the
way that modern Christians should think theologically about
their health problems.

Second, I think it is extremely important to distinguish
between "faith" and "superstition." I am by no means
suggesting that you are guilty of superstition. But I do think,
judging only from what you say in your post, that some
conceptual distinctions here might be helpful as you seek to
think about your health problems in a spiritually mature way.
So here goes:

Faith is the trust that God is present with us whatever our
difficulties may be, and indeed, that our difficulties should
be seen in part as opportunities to discover God's presence.
That is precisely what "healing rituals" such as those
described in the Epistle of James and practiced by your
church are intended to do. They help Christians discover
God's compassion and presence in the midst of their trials;
they teach them, as it were, *how* to be sick in a Christianly
faithful way. Of course, it is perfectly permissible for devout
Christians to pray for a cure to their illnesses. But they will
also have recourse to the best medical services available,
confident that God works through those services (though not
only through those services) to carry out his loving purposes
for his children.

In contrast, superstition is the attempt to get God to do our
bidding, under the assumption that God's responsiveness
to our petitions somehow depends on our uttering the "right"

words or performing the "proper" gestures and ceremonies. Some people are so superstitious that they even think that it is wrong for them to use medical services in conjunction with their prayers, as if doing so would imply a lack of faith in God. In fact, refusing to use the available medical services in preference for "miracle cures" is really a way of tempting God, of daring God to act as we would have him act, and of implying that we think that God must act if we go through the right "religious" motions. (Whatever their intentions may be, I suspect that some TV "faith healers" seduce viewers into thinking that if they *don't* get well after watching the show and sending the donation, they must lack faith, and that if they only had *more* faith and sent in *more* money they *would* get well. That only piles guilt on top of people's pain and is dreadfully wrong!)

So please do not think that there is any magical formula for being healed of whatever disease you may have. And please do continue to pray for healing and to attend the healing services your church offers. And please continue, also, to follow your doctor's advice, because s/he is among the agents that God is using to convey his love and care to you. Finally, please understand that although there is certainly no "point in suffering" unnecessarily, a Christian must never forget that God can use all things, including suffering, to reveal his love and wisdom to us.

In Christian service,

RBS

NOTES

1 At the time I was writing these paragraphs, the Seattle Seahawks football team was enjoying great success and headed for the playoffs. In that context one of our local newspapers ran an article titled, "Does God want your team to win?" (Rachel Zoll, *Seattle Times* [27 December, 2005], E-1.) No one with proper theological training would even *ask* that question, though it is certainly the task of the theologian to respond to students—and sometimes to journalists—who *do* ask such howlers. It is but small consolation that the article's subtitle read: "Well, probably not. But faith and sports are sometimes hard to separate." With delicate irony, Ms. Zoll has given us the "right" answer to what is certainly a wrongly posed question.

2 When the so-called "problem of evil" comes up, I often tell my students of an experience I had many years ago when I was a summer pastor in Vermont. My supervisor had sent me to visit a woman who had not been in church for several months—not since her two-year-old son had died of some horrible, inexplicable wasting disease. She had looked me in the eye and asked me this question. I replied: "I don't know why God let your baby die. But if I did know, I wouldn't tell you. For I respect you too much to try to replace your son with pious formulas. His death was a tragedy. It deserves tears, not explanation." The story is told in greater detail in "All or Nothing: Reflections on the Suffering of Children," *Stauros Notebook* 17/4 (Christmas, 1998), 1–4. This is the article to which I refer in my reply to Alison's post.

3 Young Life is an Evangelical Christian para-church program for high school students. Many SPU students and recent graduates work as counselors for Young Life groups. Open Door is a specialized program for high school students with mental and physical disabilities.

CHAPTER 11

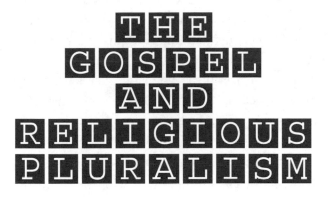

THE GOSPEL AND RELIGIOUS PLURALISM

When I was a student at Yale Divinity School, I regularly attended the Eucharist service that Fr. Henri Nouwen celebrated daily in the campus prayer chapel. The setting was intimate: rarely were there more than twenty people present, and many of the same people came each day, so that we established quite a close-knit community. One day, as we were exchanging the kiss of peace, Nouwen leaned over to give someone a hug and accidentally knocked over the chalice of consecrated wine. His face went white as a sheet, and he muttered almost inaudibly in his wonderful Dutch accent, "Zat is veddy bad." He cleaned up the spillage, refilled the cup from the pitcher, and went on with the service. But he was visibly shaken by this unintended profanation.

I learned something that day about Catholic religious sensibilities. I learned that when Catholics affirm that Christ is "really present" in the eucharistic elements, they're attesting to something they feel viscerally. I knew about the doctrine of transubstantiation when I entered the chapel that day. But what I didn't know, until witnessing that liturgical mishap, was that that doctrine tries to account philosophically for a mysterious reality that Catholics experience in the Eucharist. Seeing that opened my eyes to an aspect of Catholic worship—or rather, of *Christian worship*—that had been lost on me before. It was an "ecumenical moment" for me.

We all need to understand and appreciate religious traditions other than our own and refrain from accusing people whose beliefs and practices differ from our own of "hypocrisy" or "superstition," at least until we've studied their lives and writings. I argue that understanding another faith is learning to see it from the inside, not just the outside, learning how it *feels* to believe its teachings, obey its moral laws, practice its form of worship, and organize one's life according to its customs and calendar. My own experience in the YDS prayer chapel illustrates this. It was a big step for me, a Protestant, to study the Catholic doctrine of transubstantiation in class. It was a bigger step to begin receiving the Eucharist from a Catholic priest. But it was the biggest step of all to see the horror on that priest's face when he spilled the blood of Christ onto the stone floor. It is the same horror I feel when I hurt a friend. And *that* is precisely the point.

But it's one thing for a Protestant to learn about Catholicism. It's another thing for a Christian to learn about non-Christian religions. Indeed, the very term, "non-Christian religions," already reveals the difficulty, for it shows that we're taking Christianity as the norm by which to judge other religions. Is that really fair? Protestants and Catholics at least share the conviction that Jesus is Lord. They differ over how best to interpret and live that conviction, but with a bit of charity and imagination, they can begin to see each other's point of view. But when Christians of either sort try to extend that same charity and imagination to Jews, Muslims, Hindus, and Buddhists, a very different kind of problem arises. It seems as if they must forsake their allegiance to Jesus, or at least suspend it for a time, in order to be fair to their neighbors. Yet their reason for trying to be fair to their neighbors is because Jesus commands it.

Another paradox! As Christians, everything we say and do is supposed to be in the service of Jesus Christ, and doing anything that would diminish his preeminence would contradict our calling. Yet when, out of our love for Christ, we begin thinking that those who don't share our love for him are intrinsically inferior to us, we lapse into the kind of self-righteousness and ethnocentrism that he forbids. A reporter once asked Mahatma Gandhi what he thought of modern civilization. Gandhi said he thought it would be a good idea.[1] Christianity would be a good idea, too, especially for Christians. Before we try to convert others to our faith, we might try converting ourselves. In the process, we might try *understanding* others as best we can—for Christ's sake. And like all the other paradoxes that crop up in the study of Christian theology—and we've seen plenty, haven't we—this one is not to be solved by suppressing one side of the truth for the other, but by living both sides as faithfully as we can.

SUBJECT: CATHOLICS VS. CHRISTIANS

Dr. Steele,

I have a question regarding one of the issues that you brought up with my paper, but it's not about the actual paper. My younger brother, who is not religious in any way, shape, or form was asking me tonight about the differences between Catholics and Christians. Sure, I was able to tell him some of the obvious differences about their outward appearances and general worship styles and things, but I couldn't really go much deeper than that. Personally, it worries me that I have been subjected to both of these religions for basically all of my life and yet I stutter when trying to answer my brother's question. I know that there is a lot of background going into this and there is probably not just one simple answer, but I would really like to give my brother a real, straight answer, especially since he is asking while not currently even believing in God. I just feel so uneducated in this aspect of religion and want so much to be able to fully and honestly answer future questions of this sort. Thanks so much!

Sabrina

Dear Sabrina,

This is a wonderful question, and I want to thank you for doing me the honor of asking me. Also, I want to commend you for your concern both for your brother and for the truth, and I certainly agree that his asking the question may indicate that he is at one of those "teachable" (or "reachable") moments when a good word fitly spoken will minister to him powerfully. You are quite right, however, in saying that the answer is extremely complex and nuanced, and at the same time that he probably doesn't want to hear all the complexities and nuances. So the task of being helpful to him without being untrue to the facts is exceptionally difficult. (Welcome to the wonderful world of witnessing!) But I might put it like this:

First, it is a mistake to distinguish between "Catholics" and "Christians," because Catholics *are* Christians. That would be like distinguishing between "apples" and "fruit." Apples are a kind of fruit, and Roman Catholicism is one brand of Christianity—arguably the oldest brand, as it goes back in an unbroken line to the time of the Apostles. Certainly Catholicism is much older than Protestantism, although Protestants claim that during the late Middle Ages (the fourteenth and fifteenth centuries) Catholicism strayed from the purity of the Gospel. The Protestants took themselves to be restoring gospel truth. Of course, nowadays many Catholics openly admit that Luther, Calvin, and the other sixteenth century Reformers had a point, just as many Protestants are beginning to suspect that the Reformers threw out the baby with the bathwater. Hence ecumenical dialogue, rather than bickering, is the order of the day.

That said, one can make some generalizations about the differences in belief and worship style, but one must remember that counter-examples can be given to all of these generalizations, and that there is tremendous diversity within both camps. But for what it's worth, here are some of the main differences: (1) Protestants emphasize Scripture as the sole norm of Christian faith and practice,[2] whereas

Roman Catholics place Scripture on a par with the ancient unwritten customs of the Church. (2) Protestants deny that the unity of the church depends on the headship of any human figure (i.e., the pope) or any institution (i.e., the college of bishops, of which the pope is president). Protestants see the unity of church in the headship of Jesus Christ, and are therefore inclined to allow for a wide variety of systems of church order and governance. (3) Roman Catholics tend to understand divine grace as a kind of "thing" (e.g., an extremely rarified fluid) that somehow inheres in people (saints, especially the Blessed Virgin Mary), places (church sanctuaries and the sites of important events in Christian history, such as Jerusalem), and things (the consecrated communion elements, the relics of saints, etc.), whereas Protestants tend to understand grace "relationally," that is, as God's loving attitude toward sinners. Thus, Roman Catholicism tends to be "objectivistic," whereas Protestantism tends to be "subjectivistic." The former emphasizes the sacraments, where grace is somehow "piped" into the believer or even "consumed," while the latter emphasizes preaching, where the new relationship with God is described and people are invited to open themselves to it.[3]

Hope this helps.

RBS

SUBJECT: CAN NON-CHRISTIANS BE SAVED?

Dr. Steele,

I have a question about a topic I have discussed and talked a lot about with people, and was wondering if you could maybe help me, or point me in a direction. I am wondering about the salvation of people who are not of Christian faith. People that have never heard the gospel, or people that have had God portrayed in a negative way. What about Jews, who seek after God with the same passion that many Christians do? If you could lead me to some scripture, or things you've heard or your own convictions on this subject that would be great. Thank you very much for your time. I look forward to your response.

Kelly

Hi Kelly,

Thanks for these very thought-provoking questions. It is certainly one of the most controversial questions in theology these days, given the "shrinking" of the world through international travel and trade and the global telecommunications networks. Cultural and religious pluralism are here to stay, though of course they always were here, even if the more insulated and supposedly monolithic cultures didn't always like to admit it. My own judgment on this issue goes something like this:

1. When I preach from a Christian pulpit, I preach salvation by divine grace through faith in Jesus Christ. The salvation of non-Christians is a speculative issue, and the possibility of it seems to me just as dangerous to affirm in a dogmatic way as to deny in a dogmatic way. And since speculative issues are, in general, not the stuff of good sermons, I rarely deal with it. Nevertheless, it is certainly a hot issue, and must sometimes be addressed precisely because it's on people's minds, and they need guidance.

2. When Jesus speaks about damnation, he never says it is the certain fate of unbelievers; rather, he says it is the certain fate of hypocritical or self-righteous believers, those who are convinced of their intrinsic worthiness of salvation, and who thereby unwittingly demonstrate their *un*-worthiness. Jesus came to save sinners, not self-proclaimed saints; he sides with "the least, the last, and the lost" and he tells us within the Christian fold that there are "other sheep" whom he must seek out and gather in.

3. Despite the claim made by Cyprian of Carthage that "outside the church there is no salvation" (*extra ecclesiam nullus salus*), we know for certain that the Holy Spirit is at work "outside the church," for if that were not so, no one who is outside the church would ever come in. For we believe it is the Holy Spirit who draws them in. And if the Holy Spirit is at work in the lives of individual persons and whole cultures which have not yet been penetrated by the Gospel, who are we to deny the possibility that that work would prove "saving," even if it does not always lead to a public progression of explicit Christian faith? Again, we cannot dogmatically insist that "unbelievers" can be saved, for that would be placing arbitrary limits on the ways in which the Spirit allegedly "must" work.

4. We do not say that people are saved simply because they have a longing for God, for that would make their longing the "efficient cause" of their salvation. Rather we say that God saves persons—but also that God has placed in all persons a longing for Himself, and that God does not disappoint those whose longing for himself comes to expression in sincere religious devotion (of any sort) and in sincere acts of neighbor-love.

Hope this helps stimulate thought. If you want to pursue this or any other question, feel free to write back or stop into my office to chat.

Yours,

RBS

SUBJECT: IS CHRISTIANITY THE ONLY WAY TO GOD?

Dr. Steele,

I have a lot of thoughts and questions I would like to ask you. I hope you wouldn't mind sharing your thoughts with me on at least a few of them. I've been turning questions like these over and over in my mind for quite a long time now. And I keep wondering if, with all of these questions and uncertainties, how can we know that Christianity is the only way to God? Today, at the end of class, you said that no one can have a monopoly on the truth, yet Christians make this claim.

How do we know that God doesn't reveal Himself to people of other religions? Why wouldn't God reveal Himself to anyone except for a small group of people in a tiny part of the world? If truths are "universal," couldn't they then be universally available? Or is it that the tools for understanding these truths are not universally available? We Christians claim that the necessary "tool" is Christ? But why would that be?

Karl Barth said that all religions involve seeking God in one way or another. How do we know that the sincere seeking is not enough? In class, it seemed we ended up placing an emphasis on the quest for truth. The development of religion is present in every culture on Earth. All cultures are seeking "truth," but is anyone really finding it? We all disagree on what the ultimate truth is. Can it really be found? Are we all looking at a centrally located God from different standpoints on a circle around Him, seeing different parts and aspects of Him? Can we claim that Muslims, Hindus, etc. will not be "saved"? But I see the danger in that viewpoint. It would cause us to become lackadaisical, to not attempt to share the Gospel with others. It allows a spirit of relativism to sink in, preventing us from seeking the "universal" truths that must be lurking out there. But I still have a hard time with all these ideas. I feel like there is a gigantic web of stuff and God in His fullness of truth is on one side, and humanity is on the other. This makes it difficult to know what we should be like, though, to know what universal "goods" (if there are any) to strive for. It makes it tough to know what God wants us to be like. I don't know what to do with all of this.

Thanks,

Kelsey

Dear Kelsey,

Thanks for these profound questions and meditations. Let me respond to each of your paragraphs in turn. First, I am not convinced that Christians really do claim to have a monopoly on the truth, or at least that we must or ought to do so. Certainly Christians are committed to the belief that God has revealed himself uniquely and decisively in Jesus of Nazareth. But that is not the same as claiming that God has revealed himself *only* in Jesus Christ, or that the truth claims of all other religions are necessarily false.

Therefore I see no reason to think that all "other" religions besides Christianity are simply false. That idea would seem to imply that the Holy Spirit operates solely within the confines of the Church. And such an implication is plainly false, since we want to assert that it is the Holy Spirit who draws people who are outside the church into a saving relationship with God through Jesus, usually by drawing them into the fellowship of the church. The question is, can the Holy Spirit draw people who are outside the church into a saving relationship with God without drawing them into the kind of relationship with Jesus and participation in the church that Christians take to be normative? I do insist that the profession of faith in Jesus as Lord and Savior and active membership in the church really are the normal and normative way for persons to attain salvation, but I am unwilling to assert that they are the only way, for that would "tie the hands" of the Spirit in a manner which seems to me theologically objectionable.

As to the relativism so popular today, I am certainly no fan of it. Indeed, in a curious way, such relativism often proves on examination to be curiously absolutistic. For it holds that "truth" is relative—absolutely all truth. But if absolutely all truth is relative, then the statement that all truth is relative cannot itself be absolutely true. You can see that this line of thinking piles self-contradiction on self-contradiction. At the same time, as you have already seen from the above, I am no fan of the kind of religious absolutism which denies that other religious traditions besides one's own have any access to divine truth at all. This strikes me as arrogant and self-serving, a kind of intellectual or spiritual imperialism that contradicts the Spirit of the Christian Gospel. Yet I am mindful that, as Luther and others have said, the human mind is a "factory of idols."[4] We tend to create gods in our own image, to serve our own purposes. Of course, this is as true of Christians as it is of everybody else, regardless of whether the Christian Gospel is itself true (as I believe it is).

What then are we to say about all this? Well, we are forced to say that nobody can have a perspective-free perspective on the truth, including Christians. And this is so even if we assert, as I would, that in Jesus God has acted to reveal himself to us and to disclose his ultimate intentions for us. In short, we have no "universal truths" that every reasonable and well-intentioned person on earth, regardless of nationality, language of origin, social status, religious affiliation, age-level, and gender is going to accept as soon as s/he takes an "objective" look at the "evidence." It simply doesn't work that way. Each of us must start where we are, and the Christian must recognize, like everybody else, that every account of religious truth is shaped, in part, by a particular "story" or "standpoint." But that does not mean that every account is therefore "equally true" (or "equally false"). It only means that the veracity of each account must be *shown* in the living of it, and tested by the community that holds it and professes to live it against competing accounts. I am a Christian because I am convinced that the Christian gospel finally "holds up." I believe that life lived according to the gospel, after the example and by the power of Jesus, is the most glorious, most satisfying, most honorable, and most sensible life there is. But that doesn't mean there is no glory, satisfaction, honor, or sanity in other kinds of life, and it certainly doesn't mean that all Christians live the gospel story in ways that maximize the glory, satisfaction, honor, and sanity that Christ offers.[5]

RBS

NOTES

1 E. F. Schumacher, *Good Work* (New York: Harper & Row, Publishers, 1979), 62.

2 This statement is true only of those Protestants who follow the Reformation *sola scriptura* principle. And because many SPU students come from independent Evangelical churches, it seemed safe in this context—namely a private letter to a student who attended such a church and who was looking for some elementary theological information for her brother—to peddle this gross generalization. Yet the statement is false as it stands, for there are certainly many Christians who would regard themselves as Protestants but who would not accept the *sola scriptura* principle in its strictest form. Wesleyans, for example, accept the *primacy* of Scripture among the sources

of theological knowledge, but accord ancillary roles to church tradition, human reason, and personal religious experience.

3 This generalization, too, is plainly simplistic, and may simply reinforce one of the misconceptions about Catholic doctrine that Protestants have often used to deny that Catholics are Christians—which is the very prejudice that the letter intends to correct. I therefore ask that this letter not be read as a statement of what I teach in my classes about the similarities and differences between Catholicism and Protestantism, but as a modest effort on my part to respond to a request from a very sincere student with a very delicate problem for some very basic handholds on what she herself understood was a very complex issue.

4 I was in error when I ascribed this phrase to Luther. In fact, it comes from John Calvin, *Institutes of the Christian Religion* 1:11.8.

5 For my more considered views on relativism and perspectivism, see the introduction to chapter 6 above.

Other books available from Paternoster and Authentic

For a complete catalog of Authentic publications,
please contact us at:

1-8MORE-BOOKS
ordersusa@stl.org
www.authenticbooks.com

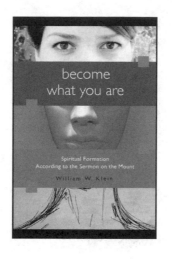

Become What You Are
Spiritual Formation According to the Sermon on the Mount

Dr. William W. Klein

If you were sitting today on a hillside listening to Jesus' Sermon on the Mount, how ought you respond? *Become What You Are* is the insider's guide to Jesus' agenda—the goal of "spiritual formation." This goal is a transformed heart, a change at the inner center of our being, that leads to a life that pleases God. Or, as a shorthand, it means becoming like Christ.

This unique approach to the most famous sermon juxtaposes "analysis" with "practice" sections throughout. In the analysis sections, the essential meaning of the text—what Jesus and Matthew were driving at—is explained for each section of the sermon. A practice section follows, calling you to engage Jesus' meaning for yourself.

By understanding what the Sermon meant in its context and how you can take it seriously in this modern world, as a follower of Jesus, you will be able to *become what you are.*

1-932805-44-3   256 Pages

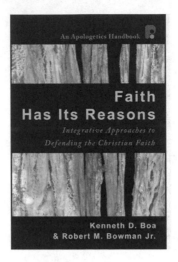

Faith Has Its Reasons
Integrative Approaches to Defending the Christian Faith:
An Apologetics Handbook

Kenneth D. Boa and Robert M. Bowman

Ever since the apostle Paul addressed the Stoic and Epicurean philosophers in Athens, relating the Christian worldview to a non-Christian world has been a challenge. And despite Peter's charge to be "ready to make a defense to everyone who asks you to give an account for the hope that is in you" (1 Peter 3:15), most Christian lay people have left apologetics—the defense of the faith—to the ecclesiastical "pros."

Faith Has Its Reasons is a study of four different models of how apologetics should be done, an assessment of their strengths and weaknesses, and a proposal for integrating the best insights of each.

1-932805-34-6   608 Pages

Read the Bible for a Change
Understanding and Responding to God's Word

Ray Lubeck

Which Bible passages are for us today and which only apply to the first ancient readers? Can we just pick and choose the verses we think fit our situation? Who gets to decide? In *Read the Bible for a Change*, Dr. Ray Lubeck helps readers correctly understand and apply the Bible to their lives. If you are serious about your relationship with God and committed to understanding His Word, this book is for you. Dr. Lubeck has devoted his life to helping people bring God's truth to their everyday life.

As professor of Bible and Theology at Multnomah Bible College, Dr. Lubeck knows what it takes to hold the interest of students of the Bible. He uses illustrations, charts, stories, and everyday examples to make learning both fun and fascinating.

1-932805-36-2   320 Pages

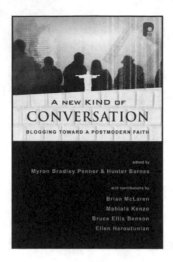

A New Kind Of Conversation
Blogging Toward a Postmodern Faith

Myron Bradley Penner and Hunter Barnes

In the midst of the cultural and intellectual upheavals of post modernity in Western society, evangelicalism finds itself in the middle of conversation about its own identity and future.

Whereas other books addressing postmodernism treat the topic in a traditional book form—an edited volume with essays—the format of this book seeks to place the discussion in a form that is consistent with its content. Using the motif of the weblog, *A New Kind of Conversation* is an experimental book that enters into this conversation with five evangelical leaders and academics (Brian McLaren, Bruce Ellis Benson, Ellen Haroutunian, Mabiala Kenzon and Myron Bradley Penner), who are the primary bloggers.

1-932805-58-3   240 Pages